# LIFE RENEWED

*By the same author*

CHRISTIAN FESTIVALS

HEAVENLY MEANINGS

JOHN PLOUGHMAN'S TALK

JOHN PLOUGHMAN'S PICTURES

LECTURES TO MY STUDENTS

MORNING AND EVENING DAILY READINGS

SIGNS AND WONDERS

THE CHEQUE BOOK OF THE BANK OF FAITH

THE TREASURY OF DAVID

THE TREASURY OF THE BIBLE

C. H. SPURGEON

# LIFE RENEWED

Sermons on Revival

LAKELAND
BLUNDELL HOUSE
GOODWOOD ROAD
LONDON SE14 6BL

Previously published in *Sermons on Revival*
(Kelvedon Edition)

© Marshall Morgan & Scott 1958

All rights reserved. No part of this publication may be reproduced, stored in a retrieval system, or transmitted in any form or by any means, electronic, mechanical, photocopying, recording or otherwise, without the prior permission of the Copyright owner.

*This edition 1972*

ISBN 0 551 00287 5

Printed in Great Britain by
Lowe & Brydone (Printers) Ltd., London

# CONTENTS


*page*

1. Man's Extremity, God's Opportunity (Deut. 32:36) 7
2. Revival: An Antidote for Many Ills (Ps. 80:19) 17
3. Apostolic Exhortation (Acts 3:19) 29
4. A Revival Harvest (Amos. 9:13) 41
5. Go Home and Tell Others (Mark 5:19) 53
6. Continue in Prayer (Col. 4:2) 65
7. "A People Prepared for the Lord" (Luke 1:17) 76
8. Without Christ – Nothing (John 15:5) 87
9. A Message for the Time Present (Zeph. 3:16–18) 100
10. Our Urgent Need of the Holy Spirit (Rom. 15: 13,19) 115

## 1

# MAN'S EXTREMITY, GOD'S OPPORTUNITY

"For the Lord shall judge his people, and repent himself for his servants, when he seeth that their power is gone, and there is none shut up, or left."—Deut. 32: 36.

THE same event may happen alike to all, yet it may have a very different meaning to different individuals. Ungodly men are brought low by affliction or poverty, for sinners have no immunity from suffering. Saints also are led into trying circumstances, for the utmost holiness will not preserve any man from trial. But what a difference there is between the downfall of the prosperous sinner and of the man whom God loves! The wicked man, who continueth in his wickedness, falleth for ever; but the righteous man, though he may fall seven times, riseth up again, for he shall not fall finally. How dreadful is the language of Jehovah when speaking of the ungodly! "To me belongeth vengeance, and recompence; their foot shall slide in due time: for the day of their calamity is at hand, and the things that shall come upon them make haste."

The wicked man, who prospers in this world, carries his head very high; he is proud and conceited, and he treads the poor under his feet. His career seems to be one of uninterrupted prosperity; higher, and higher, and higher, and yet higher he mounts; he becomes more wealthy and famous, and, meanwhile, he also becomes more boastful, and more arrogant towards God. He asks, "Who is the Lord that I should obey his voice?" He breathes defiance against the Most High; his heart grows harder and harder, like the heart of Pharaoh. Do you see where he is now? He has climbed to the very mountain's brow; he is rejoicing that he has reached the topmost pinnacle of fame. Who can ever pull him down from that height? Who can even disturb his peace? Wait a while, tarry but a brief season. High places are full of danger, and the terrible prophecy shall yet be fulfilled in his experience, and in that of many others who are like him. Their feet shall slide in due time"; and when men in such a position do begin to slip and slide, their fall is irrevocable. Down, down they go, falling from precipice to precipice, until they are utterly broken in pieces. Am I addressing any man who thinks that he is beyond the reach of the arrows of the Almighty? Ere another week has passed over your head, sir, you may lie gazing into eternity, and the joints of your loins shall be loosed as you begin to realize that you must so soon stand before the judgment seat of Christ. Vain, then, will be all your wealth and all your wit. You may now deride the godly, who seek mercy at the hands of God; but then, you will cry out worse than they have ever done. I would not change places with the greatest man who is living without the Saviour; if I could have the whole world given to me, if I could be the possessor of a thousand worlds, and yet live for a single moment without having my sin forgiven, and without the love of God shed abroad in my heart, it would be a living death to me.

I want you to think all the more of this solemn truth because I am going to speak of others, who do fall very low, and suffer very much, yet, after all, their descent is followed by an ascent, their declining leads to a revival, for, according to our text, "the Lord shall judge his people, and repent himself for his servants, when he seeth that their power is gone, and there is none shut up, or left."

I shall apply the text, first of all, to THE LORD'S OWN CHURCH.

It may relate to *any sorely-tried Church.* I may be addressing some brethren, up from the country, who are members of churches that are sadly declining. If that is the case, let me remind you, dear friends, that God may have a true church which is very severely tried. The track of the ship of the Church has lain full often over very boisterous waters. Sometimes the sea has seethed and the billows have boiled through the fury of persecution; the prow of the vessel has been crimsoned with blood, but onward has she moved. The days of persecution have not yet ceased, but when any churches are brought very low through the attacks of cruel enemies, there is still hope for them in this promise of the living God.

What is far worse for a church even than persecution, it may be minished and brought low through the folly of its own members. Mine eyes could weep day and night over some churches that I know, which seem to me to be determined to commit spiritual suicide. They fall to quarrelling, when they are weak enough already, and need what little strength they have for fighting against the common foe. Often, they divide into parties about nothing at all; and where there should be unbroken brotherhood, there is an absence of anything like Christian love, and therefore the Spirit of God departs from them.

Many churches are, alas! brought low through a faulty ministry. A ministry that does not ring out in tones as clear as a clarion, "Salvation by grace, through faith in the precious blood of Jesus Christ," is an impoverishing ministry. If there is no nourishing food for the soul, how can it be in spiritual health? If Christ be absent from the assembly, is not everything lacking that can build up a true Christian church? In many and many a place that I wot of, the members of the church have become few and feeble because the ministry has not fed their souls. And, sometimes, a church may get down so very low that it appears as if it would become altogether extinct. One is afraid that the doors of the chapel will have to be closed, that the altar-fire will go out, and that the testimony for God will cease in that particular hamlet, or village, or township.

Now, if any of you are members of such a church as that, what you have to make sure of is that *it* is a church of Christ, and that *you* are God's people and God's servants, for our text speaks of God's favour to "his people" and "his servants." This passage does not apply to every nominal church, nor to every conglomeration of merely moral men who call themselves Christians; but it does concern every real church of God, however low it may have been brought.

When you are in such a state as this, what you have to do is to lay the condition of the Church to heart, and *to cry unto God to raise it up again.* Use every possible and right means to bring a revival; but if your way is blocked up, and there seems to be no possibility of success attending your efforts, then fall back upon this text, and plead it with God in prayer: "For the Lord shall judge his people, and repent himself for his servants, when he seeth that their power is gone, and there is none shut up, or left."

For, next, *if you pray in faith, God will return to you.* I believe that half-a-dozen persons, with vital religion in their souls, and really in earnest, may pray a church right out of any ditch into which it may have fallen, or bring it up even from the sepulchre where it has been buried, and make it live again in fulness of life; only there must be an intense determination that it shall be so, and real anguish and travail of soul until the desired end is attained. The fact that the Church has come to her extremity of weakness should cheer you, rather than drive you to despair; for when a thing is so low that it cannot get any lower, there is some consolation in that fact. Now is the time to hope that the tide will turn, and that God will raise it up again.

You remember that, when John Huss was being burned to death, he said, "Within a hundred years, there will come a man whom the persecutors will not be able to burn." The name Huss signified goose, and he said, "there will come a swan that you will never be able to roast"; that was Martin Luther, who was many times in great peril, and yet was not killed by the persecutors. When he was converted, the world was as dark spiritually as it well could be; yet God then found, even in the monastery, a monk whose preaching of the Gospel shook the world. Never be afraid of the ultimate issue of the great battle; God will beat the devil yet. If ever this pulpit should cease to resound with the Gospel of Christ, do not give up hope, my brethren; still stick together, even if there are only a few of you left, and cry mightily unto God, pleading the promise of our text, for he will remember you, and will "repent himself for his servants," and his cause shall yet again revive.

Now, in the second place, I want to show you that our text is applicable to THE TRIED BELIEVER. I may be addressing someone to whom these words of Moses shall drop as the rain, and distil as the dew.

Beloved brethren, God may bring his people, in the order of his providence, into such a state that "*their power is gone.*" Apparently, they are in such a condition that they are quite unable to help themselves. They have struggled against many difficulties; but, at last, the difficulties have proved more than a match for them. All earthly help has quite failed them; to quote the words of the text, "their power is gone, and there is none shut up, or left,"—no garrison left in the city, no soldier left in the field, no helper anywhere. You may be like Job, who had no friends left, except the miserable comforters, who spoke more like enemies than friends. You are not the first of God's servants whose power is gone, and whose friends are gone. The worst about your trial may be that it may seem to you, and seem truly, that *some of your suffering is the result of sin*. You may not have been walking with God as you ought to have done, your heart may have grown cold; so that which has come upon you may be a chastisement for your wandering, it may be a rod in the hand of your loving Father, smiting you because of your folly. But I beseech you, now that all human power is gone, do not run away from God, but fly to him. Do not give up your hope in him. However deplorable your circumstances may be, let them drive you to God, and not from him. Your only hope now lies in the compassion of your God. Let me read this text again to you, and I pray that your faith may enable you to grasp it: "for the Lord shall judge his people, and repent himself for his servants, when he seeth that their power is gone, and there is none shut up, or left." There is a gracious purpose behind your present trial, even though you do not yet perceive it.

It is possible that it was absolutely necessary that you should be brought as low as you are *in order to cure you of your sin*. You have come to your last shilling, have you? I have known a doctor to keep his patient almost without food, and bring the man down very low in order to starve out the complaint from which he was suffering; and in a surgical case, the knife has had to go in very deeply so as to get at the roots of the cancer. In like manner, it may be that it was necessary that your affliction should not be stopped midway, but should be allowed to proceed to the bitter end, in order that it might be the means of curing you of the evils which were rankling in your spirit.

Possibly, too, the affliction was permitted to develop to the uttermost *in order that you might be induced to return to your God*. It may be that, in your prosperity, you had grown so careless and so fond of the world, and you had so little delight in God, that it was necessary for you to have your gourds withered, and your flowers all made to decay, in order that you might, in your abject distress, turn again unto your God.

Or it may be that God intends that *you should for ever bear a testimony to his faithfulness such as no ordinary man can bear.* Those people who only sail in a little boat on a lake have no stories to tell of adventures at sea; but he who is to write a book describing long voyages must travel far out of sight of land, and behold the sea in the time of storm, as well as in a calm. You are to become, perhaps an experienced Christian, you are to bring great honour to God, by being the means of comforting others who will be tried in a similar way to yours, you are to be trained into a hero, and that cannot be done except by great and bitter griefs coming upon you. I believe that there are some of us whom God cannot trust with much joy. His head would turn dizzy if he were set upon a high pinnacle, and he would get proud, and self-sufficient, and so be ruined. God will not kill his children with sweets any more than he will destroy them with bitters. They shall have a tonic when they need it; but when that tonic is so bitter that they seem as if they could not drink it and live, their Lord will either take the tonic away, or give them some delicious sweetness to remove all the bitter taste.

I will read the text to you again; I cannot preach from it as I should like to do, but the text itself is full of comfort to the Lord's own chosen ones who are in sore straits: "For the Lord shall judge his people, and repent himself for his servants, when he seeth that their power is gone, and there is none shut up, or left." Tried child of God, I wish I could grasp thy hand in tenderest sympathy, and whisper in thine ear, "In thy lowest moments, do not despair. 'Hath God forgotten to be gracious? hath he in anger shut up his tender mercies?' Nay, verily, 'for the Lord will not cast off for ever: but though he cause grief, yet will he have compassion according to the multitude of his mercies.' 'Weeping may endure for a night, but joy cometh in the morning.' The Lord himself saith to thee, 'I have loved thee with an everlasting love: therefore with lovingkindness have I drawn thee;' 'when thou passest through the waters, I will be with thee; and through the rivers, they shall not overflow thee: when thou walkest through the fire, thou shalt not be burned; neither shall the flame kindle upon thee.' Therefore, if thou walkest in darkness, and seest no light, trust in the Lord, and stay thyself upon thy God, for he will have compassion upon thee; he will take away his wrath, and smile again upon thy soul, and turn thy lamentation into singing, and thy mourning into dancing."

I want secondly to show that the text also applies to THE CONVICTED SINNER.

Are there any of you who cannot say that you are the children of God, but who wish that you were? I said to one, the other day, "Are you a Christian?" and he replied, "No, sir; but, oh! how I wish that I were!" When I heard with what emphasis he spoke, I thought that he must be not far from the kingdom; for is not he who wishes to be a Christian, almost one already? Is there not the beginning of a work of grace in his heart which the Holy Spirit will carry on to completion? So I will read the text now to you who wish to be saved, but fear that you shall not be, for you have such a dreadful sense of sin: "For the Lord shall judge his people, and repent himself for his servants, when he seeth that their power is gone, and there is none shut up, or left."

Do these words describe your present condition? First, *is your self-righteousness all gone?* A few months ago, you were a fine fellow according to your own estimate; you thought that there were few as good as you. But, you came slinking in as if you felt afraid even to sit down with the people of God. You remember that line of the hymn, "Then look, sinner,—look unto him, and be saved," and you feel that you would like to look to the Crucified One; you can go as far as that, but you cannot yet say that you have looked unto him, and that you are saved, for you have such an awful sense of your guilt in the sight of God. I know you, my friend; I "know the heart of a stranger"; for such was my heart in the time of my conviction on account of sin. Oh, the heaviness of a guilty conscience! Oh, the long, dark, dreary winter of the soul, when sin blots out the sun, turns even mercy into misery, and sorrow makes the day into night! Ah! I know you, my brother; your self-righteousness is all gone, and I am glad of it.

Then, next, you say that *your power is all gone.* Not many months ago, you thought that you could believe in the Lord Jesus Christ whenever you liked, that it was the easiest thing in all the world to become a Christian, and that you would trust the Saviour, some fine day or other, whenever you pleased. Yet, at this moment, you are sighing, "I would, but can't believe. Lord, relieve my load of guilt. All my help must come from thee." You are the gentleman who was going to conquer his evil temper, and give up his bad habits, and be a saint, and do it all yourself! Oh, yes, yes! then, you thought you could do anything and everything, but now you have come to realize that, apart from Christ, you can do nothing. Only the other morning, when you got up, you prayed to God, and you thought that you would lead a very good life throughout that whole day, yet you were out of temper before breakfast was over. You went to your business, and you were going to be quite an example there; and a pretty example you were! You felt that, as you went home at night, all your attempts to be better, and to do right, had failed. I am glad you have learnt your weakness, and I hope that your consciousness of weakness will become deeper and more painful still; for, until every bone in your body is broken, I am afraid that you will not turn to God.

Is my text true concerning any of you? "Their power is gone, and there is none shut up, or left." Are you brought to such a pass that *you have not anything in the whole world that you dare to rely upon*? You look back upon all your church-going and your chapel-going, but you dare not rely upon them, for you feel that you have been a hypocrite in the house of God, and that your heart has not been right towards him. You look back upon your attempts to pray,—for you have been trying to pray lately,—but you feel as if you could not pray aright, the words stuck in your throat, and the very desires were dead within your spirit. Have you come to such a pass that, when you read the Bible, it condemns you; and when you hear the Gospel, the preacher seems as if he excluded you from its provisions? Is it so? Is there no ray of hope for you anywhere? You used to have some kind of hope in reserve, some secret, mysterious confidence that still buoyed you up: is that all gone? Do you realize that you are lost? Do you know that the sentence of death has been pronounced against you? Do you seem to feel in your heart the working of the Spirit, as if even now he would take you away, and cast you into hell? Blessed be the Lord if you have come to such a pass as that!

Your extremity is God's opportunity. The difficulty all along has been to get to the end of you; for when a man gets to the end of himself, he has reached the beginning of God's working. When you are cleaned right out, and have not anything at all left, then all the mercy of the covenant of grace is yours. I may have doubts about whether God's grace will be exercised in certain cases; but I cannot raise any question about the freeness of divine grace to a soul that is empty, to a soul that is ready to perish, and to a soul that is enquiring after God, to a soul that is hungering and thirsting after righteousness. When once your soul is so conscious of your sin that every hope of salvation by your own works is entirely abandoned, and you feel that you are utterly condemned, then is Jesus Christ yours, for he came, not to call the righteous, but sinners. So, accept him as yours; take him, receive him now. He is made of God fulness to our emptiness, righteousness to our unrighteousness, life to our death, salvation to our condemnation, all in all to our poverty, our wretchedness, our sin.

Now let me read the text to you yet once more, and see if God the Holy Spirit does not press it home upon your conscience and heart: "For the Lord shall judge his people, and repent himself for his servants, when he seeth that their power is gone, and there is none shut up, or left." There is no hope for you except in the pity of God, no hope except in his mercy, and no hope of mercy except in the freeness of his mercy; and no hope even of the freeness of mercy except in the sovereignty of God, who hath mercy on those upon whom he will have mercy, and who gives his grace to the most unworthy, that it may be proved to be all the greater grace because it saves the very chief of sinners. If there is one of you who says, "I am the most unlikely man in all the world ever to be saved; I have the least claim upon God of any man that lives; the only claim I have is the right to be damned, for I have so grievously transgressed against God; I feel myself to be so guilty, that my only claim upon justice is the demand to be tried, condemned, and executed";—if you really mean what you say, then you are the man to whom the Gospel of the grace of God is specially sent, for it is written, "when we were yet without strength, in due time Christ died for the ungodly. For scarcely for a righteous man will one die: yet peradventure for a good (a benevolent) man some would even dare to die. But God commendeth his love toward us, in that, while we were yet sinners, Christ died for us." He gave himself for our sins, not for our righteousness; and he himself said, "They that are whole have no need of the physician, but they that are sick: I came not to call the righteous, but sinners to repentance." Trust Christ, thou who darest not trust thyself. Fling thyself, all broken to pieces, at the feet of the broken-hearted Saviour, and he will turn again, and have compassion upon you. Yea, look unto him, and live, for—

*There is life for a look at the Crucified One:*
*There is life at this moment for thee.*

Give but one believing glance at that dear dying Son of God, and thou shalt hear him say to thee, "Go thy way; thy sins, which are many, are all forgiven thee." The Lord grant it, for his name's sake! Amen.

## 2

## AN ANTIDOTE FOR MANY ILLS

"Turn us again, O Lord God of hosts, cause thy face to shine; and we shall be saved."—Ps. 80: 19.

THIS seems to be the only prayer the Psalmist puts up in this Psalm, as being of itself sufficient for the removal of all the ills over which he mourned. Though he sighs over the strife of neighbours and the ridicule of foes; and lamenting the ill condition of the goodly vine, he deplores its broken hedges, and complains of the wild beasts that waste and devour it, yet he does not petition the Most High against these evils in detail; but gathering up all his wishes into this one prayer, he reiterates it o'er and o'er—"Turn us again, O Lord God of hosts, cause thy face to shine; and we shall be saved." The reason is obvious. He had traced all the calamities to one source, "O Lord God, how long wilt thou be angry—?" And now he seeks refreshing from one fountain. Let thy face no longer frown, but let it beam upon us with a smile and all shall then be well.

THE BENEFITS OF REVIVAL TO ANY CHURCH IN THE WORLD WILL BE A LASTING BLESSING.

God's revivals, whilst they are attended with a great heat and warmth of piety, yet have with them knowledge as well as life, understanding as well as power. The revivals that we may consider to have been genuine, were such as those wrought by the instrumentality of such men as President Edwards in America, and Whitefield in this country, who preached a free-grace Gospel in all its fulness. Such revivals I consider to be genuine, and such revivals, I repeat again, would be a benefit to any church under heaven. There is no church, however good it is, which might not be better; and there are many churches sunken so low, that they have abundant need, if they would prevent spiritual death, to cry aloud, "Lord, revive us."

Among the blessings of the revival of Christians, we commence, by noticing *the salvation of sinners.* When God is pleased to pour out his Spirit upon a church in a larger measure than usual, it is always accompanied by the salvation of souls. And oh, this is a weighty matter, to have souls saved. Some laugh, and think the salvation of the soul is nothing; but I trust you know so much of the value of souls that you will ever think it to be worth the laying down of your lives, if you might but be the means of the saving of one single soul from death. The saving of souls, if a man has once gained love to perishing sinners, and love to his blessed Master, will be an all-absorbing passion to him. It will so carry him away, that he will almost forget himself in the saving of others. He will be like the stout, brave fireman, who careth not for the scorch or for the heat, so that he may rescue the poor creature on whom true humanity hath set his heart. He must, he will pluck such an one from the burning, at any cost and expense to himself. Oh the zeal of such a man as that Whitefield to whom I have alluded! He says in one of his sermons, "My God, I groan day-by-day over the salvation of souls. Sometimes," he says, "I think I could stand on the top of every hackney-coach in the streets of London, to preach God's Word. It is not enough that I can do it night and day, labouring incessantly by writing and by preaching; I would that I were multiplied a thousand-fold, that, I might have a thousand tongues to preach this Gospel of my blessed Redeemer."

Ah, you find too many Christians who do not care about sinners being saved. The minister may preach, but what heed they the results? So long as he has a respectable congregation, and a quiet people it is enough. I trust, my friends, we shall never sink to so low a state as to carry on our services without the salvation of souls. I have prayed my God many a time, and I hope to repeat the prayer, that when I have no more souls to save for him, no more of his elect to be gathered home, he may allow me to be taken to himself, that I may not stand as a cumberground in his vineyard, useless, seeing there is no more fruit to be brought forth.

I know you long for souls to be converted. I have seen your glad eyes when, at the church-meetings, night after night, sinners have told us what the Lord has done for them. I have marked your great joy when drunkards, blasphemers, and all kinds of careless persons have turned with full purpose of heart unto God, and led a new life. Now, mark you, if these things are to be continued, and above all, if they are to be multiplied, we must have again a revival in our midst. For this we must and will cry, "O Lord our God, visit thy plantation, and pour out again upon us thy mighty Spirit."

Another effect of a revival in a church is generally *the promotion of true love and unanimity in its midst.* An active church will be a united church; a slumbering church will be sure to be a quarrelsome one. If any minister desires to heal the wounds of a church, and bring the members into unanimity, let him ask God to give them all enough to fill their hands; and when their hands are full of their Master's work and their mouths are full of his praise, they will have no time for devouring one another, or filling their mouths with slander and reproach. Oh that Christ would give us that spirit that loveth all, hopeth for all, and will bear burdens for all, passing by little things, and differences of judgment and opinion, that so we may be united with a threefold cord that cannot be broken.

A revival is also necessary *in order that the mouths of the enemies of the truth may be stopped.* Do they not open wide their mouths against us? Ay, and not only against us, but against the truth we preach, and against the God we honour. How shall their mouths be stopped? By our replying to them? No; foul scorn we think it to utter one single word in our own defence. If our conduct be not sufficiently upright to commend itself, we will not utter words in order to commend it. But the way we can shut our adversaries' mouths is this: by seeking a revival in our midst. What! do they rail against our ministry? If more souls are saved, can they rail against that? Ay, let them if they will. Do they speak against the doctrines? Let them; but let our lives be so holy that they must lie against us when they dare to say that our doctrines lead any into sin. Let us seek of God that we may be so earnest, so eminently holy, so God-like, and so Christ-like, that to all they say their own consciences may tell them, "Thou utterest a falsehood whilst thou speakest against him." This was the glory of the Puritans: they preached doctrines which laid them open to reproach. I am bold to say I have preached the doctrine of the Puritans; and I am bold to say, moreover, that those parts which have been most objected to in my discourses, have frequently been quotations from ancient fathers, or from some of the Puritans. I have often smiled when I have seen them condemned, and said, "There now, sir, thou hast condemned Charnock, or Bunyan, or Howe, or Doddridge," or some other saint of God whom it so happened I quoted at the time. The word condemn was theirs, and therefore it did not so much affect me. They were held up to reproach when they were alive; and how did they answer their calumniators? By a blameless and holy life. They, like Enoch, walked with God; and let the world say what they would of them, they only sought to keep their families the most rigidly pious, and themselves the most strictly upright in the world; so that while it was said of their enemies, "They talk of good works," it was said of the Puritans, that "They did them"; and while the Arminians, for such they were in those days, were living in sin, he who was called Calvinist, and laughed at, was living in righteousness, and the doctrine that was said to be the promoter of sin was found afterwards to be the promoter of holiness. We defy the world to find a holier people than those who have espoused the doctrines of free-grace, from the first moment until now. Their faith let us follow, and their charity let us emulate. Let us seek a revival here.

Above all, we want a revival, *if we would promote the glory of God*. The proper object of a Christian's life is God's glory. The Church was made on purpose to glorify God; but it is only a revived Church that brings glory to his name. Think you that all the churches honour God? I tell you nay; there are some that dishonour him—not because of their erroneous doctrines, nor perhaps because of any defect in their formalities, but because of the want of life in their religion. There is a meeting for prayer; six people assemble beside the minister. Does that proclaim your homage to God? Does that do honour to Christianity? Go ye to the homes of these people; see what is their conversation when they are alone; mark how they walk before God. Go to their sanctuaries and hear their hymns; there is the beauty of music, but where is the life of the people? Listen to the sermon; it is elaborate, polished, complete, a master-piece of oratory. But ask yourselves, "Could a soul be saved under it, except by a miracle? Was there anything in it adapted to stir men up to goodness? It pleased their ears; it instructed them in some degree, perhaps, but what was there in it to teach their hearts?" Ah, God knows there are many such preachers. Notwithstanding their learning and their opulence, they do not preach the Gospel in its simplicity, and they draw not near to God our Father. If we would honour God by the Church, we must have a warm Church, a burning Church, loving the truths it holds, and carrying them out in the life. Oh that God would give us life from on high, lest we should be like that Church of old of whom it was said, "Thou hast a name to live, and art dead."

WHAT ARE THE MEANS OF REVIVAL? They are two-fold. One is, "Turn us again, O Lord God of hosts"; and the other is, "Cause thy face to shine." There can be no revival without both of these. "Turn us again, O Lord God of hosts." Your minister feels that he needs to be turned more thoroughly to the Lord his God. His prayer shall be, God helping him, that he may be more fearless and faithful than ever; that he may never for one moment think what any of you will say with regard to what he utters, but that he may only think what God his Master would say concerning him;—that he may come into the pulpit with this resolve—that he cares no more for your opinion with regard to the truth than if you were all stones, only resolving this much:—come loss or come gain by it, whatsoever the Lord God saith unto him, that he must speak; and he desires to ask his Master that he may come here with more prayer himself than heretofore, that whatever he preaches may be so burnt into his own soul that you may all know, even if you do not think it true yourselves, that at any rate he believes it, and believes it with his inmost soul. And I will ask of God that I may so preach to you, that my words may be attended with a mighty and a divine power. I do forswear all pretence to ability in this work. I forswear the least idea that I have aught about me that can save souls, or anything which could draw men by the attractions of my speech. I feel that if you have been profited by my preaching, it must have been the work of God, and God alone, and I pray to him that I may be taught to know more my own weakness. Wherein my enemies say aught against me, may I believe what they say, but yet exclaim,

*Weak though I am, yet through his might,*
*I all things can perform.*

Will you ask such things for me, that I may be more and more turned to God, and that so your spiritual health may be promoted?

But there are some of you who are workers in the Church. Large numbers are actively engaged for Christ. In the Sabbath School, in the distribution of tracts, in preaching the Word in the villages, and in some parts of this great city—many of you are striving to serve God. Now what I ask and exhort you to is this: cry unto God—"Turn us again, O God." You want, my dear working friends, more of the Spirit of God in all your labours. I am afraid we forget him too much; we want to have a greater remembrance of him. Sunday School teachers, cry unto God that you may attend your classes with a sincere desire to promote God's glory, leaning wholly on his strength. Do not be content with the ordinary routine, gathering your children there, and sending them home again; but cry, "Lord, give us the agony which a teacher ought to feel for his child's soul." Ask that you may go to the School with deep feelings, with throes of love over the children's hearts, that you may teach them with tearful eyes, groaning before heaven that you may be the means of their salvation and deliverance from death. And you who in other ways serve God, I beseech you do not be content with doing it as you have done. You may have done it well enough to gain some approval of your fellows: do it better, as in the sight of the Lord. I do not mean better as to the outward form, but better as to the inward grace that goeth with it. Oh! seek from God that your works may be done from pure motives, with more simple faith in Christ, more firm reliance on him, and with greater prayer for your success. "Turn us again," is the cry of all, I hope, who are doing anything for Jesus.

Others of you are intercessors; and here I hope I have taken in all who love the Lord in this place. Oh! how much the strength of a church depends upon these intercessors! I had almost said we could do better without the workers than the intercessors. We want in every church, if it is to be successful, intercessors with God—men who know how to plead with him and to prevail.

We do want more prayer. Your prayers, I am sure, have been more earnest at home than ever they were, during the last three weeks; let them be more earnest still. It is by prayer we must lean on God; it is by prayer that God strengthens us. I beseech you, wrestle with God. I know your love to one another, and to his truth. Wrestle with God, in secret and in public, that he would yet open the windows of heaven, and pour out a blessing upon us, such as we shall not have room enough to receive. There must be a turning again to God of the intercessors in prayer.

Again: we want a turning again to God of all of you who have been accustomed to hold communion with Jesus, but who have in the least degree broken off that holy and heavenly habit. Beloved, are there not some of you who were accustomed to walk with God each day? Your morn was sanctified with prayer, and your eventide was closed in with the voice of praise. You walked with Jesus, in your daily business; you were real Enochs; you were Johns; you did lay your head on the bosom of your Lord. But ah! have not some of you known suspended communion of late? Have not we ourselves held less communions with Jesus? Have not our prayers been fewer to him, and his revelations less bright to us? It will never do for us to live without communion; we cannot, we must not, we dare not live without constant hourly fellowship with Jesus. I would stir you up in this matter. Seek of God that you may return, and experience the loveliness of Jesus in your eyes, that you may know more and more of your loveliness in his eyes.

And once more, beloved, "Turn us again" must be the prayer of you all, not only in your religious labours, but in your daily lives. Oh! how I do groan over each one of you, especially those of you who are my children in Christ, whom God has granted me to be the means of bringing from nature's darkness into marvellous light; that your lives may be an honour to your profession. Oh! my dear hearers, may none among you who make a profession, be found liars to God and man. There are many who have been baptized, who have been baptized into the waters of deception; there are some who put the sacramental wine between their lips, who are a dishonour and a disgrace to the church in which they assemble. Some who sing praises with us here can go and sing the songs of Satan elsewhere. You have crept into our number, you have deceived us, and there you are, like a cancer in our midst. God forgive you, and change your hearts; God turn you to himself! And one and all of us, though we hope we have the root of the matter in us, yet how much room there is for improvement and amendment! How are your families conducted? Is there as much of that true and earnest prayerfulness for your children as we could desire? How is your business conducted? Are you above the tricks of trade? Do you know how to stand aloof from the common customs of other men, and say, "If all do wrong it is no reason why I should—I must, I will do right?" Do you know how to talk? Have you caught the brogue of heaven? Can you eschew all foolishness, all filthy conversation, and seek to bear the image of Jesus Christ in the world? Cry out, ye Christians, "Turn us again, O God!" If others sin, I beseech you, do not you sin; remember how God is dishonoured by it. What! will you bring shame on Christ, and on the doctrines we profess? There is enough said against them without our giving cause of offence; lies enough are made up, without our giving any cause that men should truthfully speak ill of us. Oh! if I thought it would avail, methinks I would go down upon my knees, my brethren and sisters in Christ Jesus, to beg of you, as for my very life, that you would live close to Jesus. I do pray the Holy Spirit that he may so rest on you in every place, that your conversation may be "such as becometh the gospel of Christ."

To be personal with each other again, are we where we want to be just now, many of us? Can we put our hands to our hearts, and say "O Lord, I am, in spiritual things just where I desire to be?" No; I don't think there is one of us that could say that. Are we now what we should desire to be if we were to die in our pews? Come now, have we so lived during the past week, that we could wish this week to be a specimen-week of our whole lives? I fear not. How is your heart?—is it wholly set on Jesus? How is your faith?—doth it dwell on God alone? Is your soul sick, or is it healthy? Are you sending forth blossoms and bearing fruit, or do you feel dry and barren? Remember, blessed is the man who is planted by the rivers of water, that bringeth forth his fruit in his season. But how about yourselves? Are not some of you so cold and languid in prayer, that prayer is a burden to you? How about your trials? Do they not break your heart more, almost, than ever they did? That is because you have forgotten how to cast your burden on the Lord. How about your daily life? Have you not cause to grieve over it, as not being all you could desire it? Ah! beloved, do not reckon it a light matter to be going backwards; do not consider it a small thing to be less zealous than you used to be. Ah! it is a sad thing to begin to decline. But how many of you have done so! Let our prayer be now,—

*Lord, revive us, Lord, revive us,*
*All our help must come from thee.*

The other means of revival is a precious one—"Cause thy face to shine." Ah! beloved, we might ask of God, that we might all be devoted, all his servants, all prayerful, and all what we want to be; but it would never come without this second prayer being answered; and even if it did come without this, where would be the blessing? It is the causing of his face to shine on his Church that makes a Church flourish. Do you suppose that, if to our number there were added a thousand of the most wealthy and wise of the land, we should really prosper any the more without the light of God's countenance? Ah! no, give us our God, and we could do without them; but they would be a curse to us without him. Do you imagine that the increase of our numbers is a blessing, unless we have an increase of grace? No, it is not. It is the crowding of a boat until it sinks, without putting in any more provision, for the food of those who are in it. The more we have in numbers, the more we need have of grace. It is just this we want every day: "Cause thy face to shine." Oh! there have been times in this house of prayer, when God's face has shone upon us. I can remember seasons, when every one of us wept, from the minister down almost to the child; there have been times, when we have reckoned the converts under one sermon by scores. Where is the blessedness we once spoke of? Where is the joy we once had in this house! Brethren, it is not all gone; there are many still brought to know the Lord; but oh! I want to see those times again, when first the refreshing showers came down from heaven. Have you never heard that under one of Whitefield's sermons there have been as many as two thousand saved? He was a great man; but God can use the little, as well as the great to produce the same effect; and why should there not be souls saved here, beyond all our dreams? Ay, why not? We answer, there is no reason why not, if God does not cause his face to shine.

*If he makes bare his arm,*
*Who can his cause withstand?*
*When he his people's cause defends,*
*Who, who can stay his hand?*

Children of God, I need not enlarge on the meaning of this. You know what the shining of God's face means; you know it means a clear light of knowledge, a warming light of comfort, a living light poured into the darkness of your soul, an honourable light, which shall make you appear like Moses, when he came from the mountain—so bright, that men will scarce dare to look upon you. "Cause thy face to shine." Shall we not make this our prayer, dearly beloved? Have I one of my brethren in the faith, who will not this day go home to cry out aloud unto his God, "Cause thy face to shine?" Let us give no rest unto our God, until he hear this our prayer, "Turn us again, O Lord God of hosts, cause thy face to shine; and we shall be saved."

Come, now, let me stir you all up, all of you who love the Saviour, to seek after this revival. Some of you, perhaps, are now resolving in your hearts that you will at once, when you reach your homes, prostrate yourselves before your God, and cry out to him that he would bless his church; and oh! do so I beseech you. You have often said, when you left the house of God, "I will carry out that injunction of my pastor, and will be much in prayer." You thought to do it so soon as you arrived at home, but you did not, and so there was an untimely end of the matter—it accomplished not what was designed. Pray to God that you, as a soldier of the Cross, may never disgrace the banner under which you fight. Ask of him that you may not be like the children of Ephraim, who turned back in the day of battle, but that you may stand fast in all weathers, even as good old Jacob, when "in the day the drought consumed him and the frost by night,"—so may you serve that God who has called you with so high a calling. Perhaps others of you think there is no need of a revival, that your own hearts are quite good enough; I hope but few of you think so. But if thou dost think so my hearer, I warn thee. Thou fanciest thou art right, and therein thou dost prove that thou art wrong. He who says within himself, "I am rich and increased with goods," let him know that he is "poor, and naked and miserable." He who says he needs no revival knoweth not what he says. Beloved, you shall find that those who are noted as best among God's people need to write themselves the worst; and those who fancy all goes well in their hearts oft-times little know that an under-current of evil is really bearing them away as with a tide where they would not wish to go, whilst they fancy they are going on to peace and prosperity.

Oh! beloved, carry into effect the advice I have just given.

But oh! ye who come here and approve the truth with your judgment but yet have never felt its power in your hearts or its influence in your lives, for you we sigh and groan; for your sake I have stirred up the saints among us to pray. Oh how many of you there are that have been pricked in your consciences and hearts many a time. Ye have wept, ay, and have so wept that you have thought with yourselves "Never souls wept as we have done!" But ye have gone back again. After all the solemn warnings ye have heard, and after all the wooings of Calvary, ye have gone back again to your sins. Sinner! thou who heedest little for thyself, just hear how much we think of thee. Little dost thou know how much we groan over thy soul. Man! thou thinkest thy soul nothing; yet morning, noon, and night, we are groaning over that precious immortal thing which thou despisest. Thou thinkest it little to lose thy soul, to perish, or mayhap to be damned. Dost thou account us fools that we should cry over thee? Dost thou suppose we are bereft of reason, that we should think thy soul of so much concern, whilst thou hast so little concern for it? Here are God's people; they are crying after thy soul; they are labouring with God to save thee. Dost thou think so little of it thyself, that thou wouldst fool away thy soul for a paltry pleasure, or wouldst procrastinate thy soul's welfare beyond the limited domain of hope; Oh! sinner, sinner, if thou lovest thyself, I beesech thee, pause and think that what God's people love must be worth something; that what we labour for, and strive for, must be worth something; that what was reckoned worth a ransom so priceless as Jesus paid must have its sterling value in the sight of heaven. Do, I beseech thee, pause. Think of the value of thy soul; think how dreadful it will be if it is lost; think of the extent of eternity; think of thine own frailty; bethink thee of thine own sin, and of thy deserving. May God give thee grace to forsake thy wicked ways, turn unto him and live; for he "hath no pleasure in the death of him that dieth, but rather that he should turn unto him and live!" Therefore, saith he, "Turn thee, turn thee, why wilt thou die?"

And now, O Lord God of hosts, hear our ardent appeal to thy throne. "Turn us again." Lighten our path with the guidance of thine eye; cheer our hearts with the smiles of thy face. O God of armies, let every regiment and rank of thy militant church be of perfect heart, undivided in thy service. Let great grace rest upon all thy children. Let great fear come upon all the people. Let many reluctant hearts be turned to the Lord. Let there now be times of refreshing from thy presence. To thine own name shall be all the glory.

## 3

## APOSTOLIC EXHORTATION

"Repent ye therefore, and be converted, that your sins may be blotted out, when the times of refreshing shall come from the presence of the Lord."—Acts 3: 19.

AFTER the notable miracle of healing the lame man, when the wondering people clustered round about Peter and John, they were not at all at a loss for a subject upon which to address them. Those holy men were brimful of the Gospel, and therefore they had but to run over spontaneously, speaking of that topic which laid nearest to their hearts. To the Christian minister it should never be difficult to speak of Christ; and in whatever position he may be placed, he should never have to ask himself, "What is an appropriate subject for this people? for the Gospel is always in season, always appropriate, and if it be but spoken from the heart, it will be sure to work its way. Turning to the assembled multitude, Peter began at once to preach to them the Gospel without a single second's hesitation. Oh! blessed readiness of a soul on fire with the Spirit, Lord, grant it to us evermore. Observe how earnestly Peter turns aside their attention from himself and his brother John to the Lord Jesus Christ. "Why look ye so earnestly on us, as though by our own power or holiness we had made this man to walk?" The object of the Christian minister should always be to withdraw attention from himself to his subject, so that it should not be said, "How well *he* spake!" but, "Upon what weighty matters he treated!"

It is noteworthy that Peter, in addressing this crowd, came at once to the very essence of his message. He did not beat the bush; he did not shoot his arrow far afield, but he hit the very centre of the target. He preached not merely the Gospel of good news, but Christ, the person of Christ; Christ crucified—crucified by them, Christ risen, Christ glorified of his Father. Depend upon it, this is the very strength of the

Christian ministry, when it is saturated with the name and person and glory of the Lord Jesus Christ. If there was ever an occasion when a preacher of the Gospel might have forgotten to speak of Christ, it was surely the occasion on which Peter spake so boldly of him. For, might it not have been said, "Talk not of Jesus; they have just now haled him to the death: the people are mad against him; preach the truth, but do not mention his name. You will scarcely do good while they are so prejudiced, and you may do much mischief." But, instead of this, let them rage as they would, Peter would tell them about Jesus Christ, and about nothing else but Jesus Christ. He knew this to be the power of God unto salvation, and he would not flinch from it; so to them, even to them, he delivered the Gospel of our Lord Jesus Christ, with a pungency as well as a simplicity scarcely to be rivalled. Notice how he puts it: "*Ye*" have slain him; "*ye*" have crucified him; "*ye*" have preferred a murderer. He is not afraid of being personal; he does not shirk the touching of men's consciences; he rather thrusts his hand into their hearts and makes them feel their sin; he labours to open a window into the darkness of their spirits, to let the light of the Holy Ghost shine into their soul. Even thus, when we preach the Gospel, must we do; affectionately but graciously must we deal with men.

Nor did Peter fail, when he had enunciated the Gospel, to make the personal application by prescribing its peculiar commands. Grown up among us is a school of men who say that they rightly preach the Gospel to sinners when they merely deliver statements of what the Gospel is, and of the result of dying unsaved, but they grow furious and talk of unsoundness if any venture to say to the sinner, "Believe," or "Repent." To this school Peter did not belong—into their secret he had never come, and with their assembly, were he alive now, he would not be joined. For, having first told his hearers of Christ, of his life and death and resurrection, he then proceeds to plunge the sword, as it were up to the very hilt in their consciences by saying, "Repent ye therefore, and be converted that your sins may be blotted out." There, I say, in that promiscuous crowd, gathered together by curiosity, attracted by the miracle which he had wrought, Peter felt no hesitation, and asked no question; he preached the same Gospel as he would have preached to us today if he were here, and preached it in the most fervent and earnest style, preached the angles and the corners of it, and then preached the practical part of it, addressing himself with heart, and soul, and energy, to every one in that crowd, and saying, "Repent ye therefore, and be converted, that your sins may be blotted out."

First of all THE APOSTLE BADE MEN REPENT AND BE CONVERTED. Of this our text is proof enough without our going afield for other instances. Repent signifies, in its literal meaning, to change one's mind. It has been translated "after-wit," or "after-wisdom;" it is the man's finding out that he was wrong, and rectifying his judgment. But although that be the meaning of the root, the word has come in scriptural use to mean a great deal more. Perhaps there is no better definition of repentance than that which is given in our little children's hymn-book:

*Repentance is to leave*
*The sins we loved before,*
*And show that we in earnest grieve,*
*By doing so no more.*

Repentance is a discovery of the evil of sin, a mourning that we have committed it, a resolution to forsake it. It is, in fact, a change of mind of a very deep and practical character, which makes the man love what once he hated, and hate what once he loved. Conversion, if translated, means a turning round, a turning from, and a turning to—a turning from sin, a turning to holiness—a turning from carelessness to thought, from the world to heaven, from self to Jesus—a complete turning. The word here used, though translated in the English, "Repent and be converted," is not so in the Greek; it is really, "Repent and convert," or, rather, "Repent and turn." It is an active verb, just as the other was "Repent and turn." When the demoniac had the devils cast out of him—I may compare that to repentance; but when he put on his garments, and was no longer naked and filthy, but was said to be clothed and in his right mind, I may compare that to conversion. When the prodigal was feeding his swine, and on a sudden began to consider and to come to himself, that was repentance. When he set out and left the far country, and went to his father's house, that was conversion. Repentance is a part of conversion. It is, perhaps, I may say, the gate or door of it. It is that Jordan through which we pass when we turn from the desert of sin to seek the Canaan of conversion. Regeneration is the implanting of a new nature, and one of the earliest signs of that is, a faith in Christ, and a repentance of sin, and a consequent conversion from that which is evil to that which is good.

The apostle Peter, addressing the crowd, said to them, "Change your minds; be sorry for what you have done; forsake your old ways; be turned; become new men." That was his message as I have now put it into other words.

Now, it has been said, and said most truly, that repentance and conversion are the work of the Holy Spirit of God. You do not need that I should stop to prove that doctrine. We have preached it to you a thousand times, and we are prepared to prove that if anything be taught in Scripture, that is. There never was any genuine repentance in this world which was not the work of the Holy Spirit. For this purpose our Lord Jesus has gone on high: "He is exalted on high to give repentance and remission of sins." All true conversion is the work of the Holy Ghost. You may rightly pray in the words of the prophet, "Turn thou us, and we shall be turned;" for until God turn us, turn we never shall; and unless he convert us, our conversion is but a mistake. Hear it as a gospel summons:

*True belief and true repentance,*
*Every grace which brings us nigh;*
*Without money*
*Come to Jesus Christ and buy.*

"And yet," say you, "and yet the apostle Peter actually says to us, 'Repent, and be converted!' That is, you tell us with one breath that these things are the gift of the Holy Spirit, and then with the next breath you read the text 'Repent, and be converted.'" Ay, I do, I do, and thank God I have learned to do so. But you will say, "How reconcile you these two things?" I answer, it is no part of my commission to reconcile my Master's words: my commission is to preach the truth as I find it—to deliver it to you fresh from his hand.

I not only *believe* these things to be agreeable to one another, but I think I see wherein they do agree, but I utterly despair of making the most of men see the agreement. It shall be enough for you and for me to find what is written in Scripture, and to accept it all, whether we can see the agreement of the two sets of truths or no—to accept them both because they are both revealed. With that hand I hold as firmly as any man living, that repentance and conversion are the work of the Holy Spirit, but I would sooner lose this hand, and both, than I would give up preaching that it is the duty of men to repent and to believe, and the duty of Christian ministers to say to them, "Repent and be converted, that your sins may be blotted out." If men will not receive truth till they understand it, there are many things which they never will receive. Ay, there are many facts, common facts in nature, which nobody would deny but a fool, which yet must be denied if we will not believe them till we understand them. There is a fish fresh taken from the sea: you take it to the cook to serve it on the table. You eat salt with it, do you? What for? You will have it dried and salted, but what for? Did not it always live in the salt sea? Why then is it not salt? It is as fresh as though it had lived in the purling brooks of the upland country—not a particle of salt about it—yet it has lived wholly in the salt sea! Do you understand that? No, you cannot. But there it is, a fresh fish in a salt sea!

Do you understand it? So there may be two great truths in Scripture, which are both truths, and yet all the wise men in the world might be confounded to bring those two truths together. I do not understand, I must confess, why Moses was told to cut down a tree and put it in the bitter waters of Marah; I cannot see any connection between a tree and the water, so that the tree should make it sweet, but yet I do believe that when Moses put the tree into the water the bitterness of Marah departed, and the stream was sweet. I do not know why it is that Elisha, when he went to Jericho and found the water nauseous, said "Bring me a cruse of salt;" I do not know why his putting the salt into the stream should make it sweet—it looks to me as if it would operate the other way; but I believe the miracle, namely, that the salt was put in, and that it was sweetened.

So I do not understand how it is that my bidding impenitent sinners to repent should in any way be likely to make them do so, but I know it does—I see it every day. I do not know why a poor weak creature, saying to his fellow men, "Believe," should lead them to believe, but it does so, and the Holy Spirit blesses it, and they do believe and are saved; and if we cannot see how, if we see the fact, we will be content and bless God for it. Perhaps you may be aware that an attempt has been made by ingenious expositors to get rid of the force of this text. They have said that the repentance to which men here are exhorted is but an outward repentance. But how is it so, when it is added, "Repent and be converted, *that your sins may be blotted out*"? Does a merely outward repentance bring with it the blotting out of sin? Assuredly not. The repentance to which men are here exhorted is a repentance which brings with it complete pardon—"that your sins may be blotted out." And, moreover, it seems to me to be a shocking thing to suppose that Peter and John went about preaching up a hollow, outward repentance, which would not save men. It was a soul-saving repentance, and nothing less than that, which Peter commanded of these men.

Now, let us come to the point. We tell men to repent and believe, not because we rely on any power in them to do so, for we know them to be dead in trespasses and sins; not because we depend upon any power in our earnestness or in our speech to make them do so, for we understand that our preaching is less than nothing apart from God; but we find that, if we speak in faith, God the Holy Ghost operates with us, and while we bid the dry bones live, the Spirit makes them live—while we tell the lame man to stand on his feet, the mysterious energy makes his ankle-bones to receive strength—while we tell the impotent man to stretch out his hand, a divine power goes with the command, and the hand is stretched out and the man is restored. The power lies not in the sinner, not in the preacher, but in the Holy Spirit, which works effectually with the Gospel by divine decree, so that where the truth is preached the elect of God are quickened by it, souls are saved, and God is glorified. Go on preaching the Gospel boldly, and be not afraid of the result, for, however little may be your strength, and though your eloquence may be as nought, yet

God has promised to make his Gospel the power to save, and so it shall be down to the world's end.

In the second place, THERE WAS GOOD REASON FOR THIS COMMAND.

The text says, "Repent ye *therefore.*" The apostle was logical: he had a reason for his exhortation. It was not mere declamation, but sound reasoning. "Repent ye therefore." What, then, was the argument? Why, first, because you, like the Jews, have put Jesus Christ to death. This was literally true of the people to whom he spoke: they had had a share in Christ's execution. And this is spiritually true of you today. Every sin in the essence of it is a killing of God. Do you comprehend me? Every time you do what God would not have you do, you do in effect, so far as you can, put God out of his throne, and disown the authority which belongs to his Godhead; you do in intent, so far as you can, kill God. That is the drift of sin—sin is a God-killing thing. When our Lord Jesus Christ was nailed to the tree by sinners, sin only did then literally and openly what all sin really does in a spiritual sense.

Suppose the principle of thy disobedience were carried out to the full, would not all laws be disregarded, and moral government subverted? And why not, since what one may do another has clearly the same right to do? What, then, if the authority of God should be no more owned in the universe—where should we all be? What a hell above ground would this world become! Do you not see what a mischievous thing, then, your iniquity has been? Repent and turn from it. If you can really believe that though you did not nail Christ to the cross, nor plait the crown of thorns and put it on his head, nor stand and mock him there, yet that every sin is a real crucifixion of Christ, and a mockery of Christ, and a slaughter of Christ. Then, truly, there is abundant reason why you should repent and turn from it.

The apostle also used another argument, namely, that he whom they had slain was a most blessed person—one so blessed that God the Father had exalted him. Jesus Christ came not into this world with any selfish motive, but entirely out of philanthropy, full of love to men; and yet men put him to death? Now, every sin is an insult against the good and kind God. God does not deserve that we should rebel against him. If he were a great tyrant domineering over us, putting us to misery, there might be some excuse for our sin, but when he acts like a tender father to us, supplying our wants day by day, and forgiving our offences, it is shame, a cruel shame that we should live in daily revolt against him. You who have not believed in Christ, have mighty cause for repenting that you have not believed in him, seeing he is so good and kind. What hurt has he ever done you that you should curse at him? What injury has Jesus done to any of you that you should despise him?

Moreover, Peter used another plea, that while they had rejected the blessed Christ they had chosen a murderer. Sinner, thou hast despised Christ, and what is it thou hast chosen? Has it been the drunkard's cup? Oh, what a bestial thing to prefer to Christ! Or has it been thy lust? What a devilish thing to set in the place of Christ! Man, what have thy sins done to thee that thou shouldst prefer them to Jesus? Have you lived in them for years? then what wages have you had? what profit have you had? Tell me now, you that have done the farthest in sin, tell me now, are you satisfied with the service? Would you wish to go over again the days you have lived, and to reap in your own bodies the fruit of your misdeeds? Nay, but you serve a hard master; a murderer from the beginning is that devil to whom you surrender your lives. Oh, then, this is a thing to be repented of—that you have cast Christ away, but have chosen a murderer. "Not this man," say you, "but Barabbas." You will take this murderous world, this killing sin, but the blessed Saviour, you let him go. Is not there good argument here for repentance and conversion? Surely there is.

Peter clinches his reasoning with another argument, bringing down, if I may so say, the big hammer this time upon the head of the nail. It is this, that the Lord Christ, whom you have hitherto despised, is able to do great things for you. "His name through faith in his name hath made this man strong, whom ye see and know." Christ then, by faith in him, is able to do for you all that you want. If you will trust Jesus today, all your iniquities shall be blotted out; the past shall not be remembered; the present shall be rendered safe, and the future blessed. If thou trustest in Christ, there is no sin which he will not forgive thee, no evil habit the power of which he will not break, no foul propensity the weight of which he cannot remove. Believing in him, he can make thee blessed beyond a dream. And is not this cause for repentance, that thou shouldst have slighted one who can do thee so much good? With hands loaded with love he stands outside the door of your heart. Is not this good reason for opening the door and letting the Heavenly Stranger in, when he can bless you to such a vast extent of benediction? What, will you reject your own mercies? Will you despise the heaven which shall be yours if you will have my Master? Will you choose the doom from which none but he can rescue you, and let go the glory to which none but he can admit you?

There was one other plea which he used, which I would employ now. He said, "Brethren, I wot that through ignorance ye did it." As if he would say, "Now that ye have more light, repent of what you did in the dark." So might I say to some here present. You had not heard the Gospel, you did not know that sin was so bad a thing, you did not understand that Jesus Christ was able to save to the uttermost them that came unto God by him. Well, now you do understand it. The times of your ignorance God winks at, but now, "commandeth all men everywhere to repent." Greater light brings greater responsibility. Do not go back to your sin, lest it become tenfold sin to you; for if you do in the light what once you did in the darkness, he who winked at you when you knew no better, may lift his hand, and swear that you shall never enter into his rest, because you sinned presumptuously, and did despite to the Spirit of his grace. I charge every unconverted man here to mind what he is at in future. If he did not know that Jesus was able to save him before, he knows it now; if he was in the dark till today, he is not in the dark any longer. "Now ye have no cloak for your sin." Therefore, because the cloak is pulled away, and you sin against the light, I say as Peter did, "Repent and be converted, that your sins may be blotted out."

But now, our third remark shall be given with brevity, and it is this, THAT WITHOUT REPENTANCE AND CONVERSION, SIN CANNOT BE PARDONED.

The expression used in the text, "blotted out," in the original may be better explained in this way. Many Oriental merchants kept their accounts on little tablets of wax. On these tablets of wax, they indented marks which recorded the debts, and when these debts were paid, they took the blunt end of the stylus or pencil, and just flattened down the wax, and the account entirely disappeared. That was the form of "blotting out" in those days. Now, he that repents and is pardoned, is, through the precious blood of Christ, so entirely forgiven, that there is no record of his sin left. It is as though the stylus had levelled the marks in the wax, and there was no record left. What a beautiful picture of the forgiveness of sin! It is all gone, not a trace left.

But rest assured it cannot be removed except there be repentance and conversion as the result of faith in Jesus. This must be so, for this is most seemly. Would you expect a great king to forgive an erring courtier unless the offender first confessed his fault! Where is the honour and dignity of the throne of God, if men are to be pardoned while as yet they will not confess their sin? In the next place, it would not be moral; it would be pulling up the very sluices of immorality to tell men that they could be pardoned while they went on in their sins and loved them. What, a thief pardoned and continue to thieve! Truly, then, the Gospel would be the servant of unrighteousness, and against us who preach it morality should make a law. But it is not so, impenitent sinners shall be damned, let them boast what they will about grace. Thou must hate thy sin, or God will hate thee. Thou must turn or burn. Thou canst not have thy sins and go to heaven. Which shall it be? Wilt thou leave thy sins and go to heaven, or hold thy sins and go to hell? Which shall it be, for it must be one or the other; there must be a divorce between us and sin, or there cannot be a marriage between us and Christ. Does not conscience tell us this? There is not a conscience here that will say to a man, "You can hope to be saved and yet live as you list." Some have said this—I query if any have believed it. No, no, no, blind as conscience is, and though its voice be often very feeble, yet there is enough of sight about conscience to see that continuance in sin and pardon cannot consist, and that there must be a forsaking of iniquity if there is to be a forgiving of it. Whether your conscience shall say so or not; God says it; "He that confesseth and forsaketh his sin shall find mercy," but there is no promise for the unrepenting.

If you loathe your sins, if God's Holy Spirit has made you hate your past lives, if you are anxious to be made new men in Christ Jesus, I have nothing but notes of love for you. Believe in Jesus, cast yourself on him, for he has said, "Him that cometh unto me I will in no wise cast out." "Though your sins be as scarlet, they shall be as white as snow; though they be red like crimson, they shall be as wool."

The last remark is this—REPENTANCE AND CONVERSION WILL BE REGARDED AS PECULIARLY PRECIOUS IN THE FUTURE, for my text says, "That your sins may be blotted out, *when the times of refreshing shall come from the presence of the Lord.*"

A very difficult passage indeed. Its meaning is scarcely known. Three or four meanings have been attached to it. In the first place, I think it means this—he that repents and is converted, shall enjoy the blotting out of sin in that season of sweet peace which always follows pardon. After a man has been thoroughly broken down on account of sin, God deals with him very tenderly. Amongst the very happiest parts of human life are the hours immediately after conversion. You know how we sing:

*Where is the blessedness I knew*
*When first I saw the Lord?*

When the broken bone begins to heal, David puts it, "Thou makest the bones which thou has broken to rejoice." When the prisoner first gets out of prison, when the fetters for the first time clank music as they fall broken to the ground! When the sick man leaves the sick chamber of his convictions to breathe the air of liberty, and to feel the health of a pardoned sinner! Oh, if you did but know what a bliss it is to be forgiven, you would never stay away from Christ! O "repent and be converted that your sins may be blotted out, when the times of refreshing shall come from the presence of the Lord."

Perhaps these "times of refreshing" may also relate to times of revival in the Christian Church. The only way in which you, dear friends, can share in the refreshment of a revival, is by your own repenting and being converted. A revival is a great refreshment to the Church. I pray that a mighty wave may sweep over Great Britain, for much we need it. But of what use is a revival to an unpardoned sinner? It is like the soft south wind blowing upon a corpse—it can bring no genial warmth therewith. If you repent, and be converted, then amidst the general joy of the revival, you shall have this joy, that your sins have been blotted out. What a mournful cry is that, "The harvest is past, the summer is ended, and we are not saved!" Ah! I have been praying to God that you may yet be saved now; I would fain have more conversions. It is hard preaching, it is dull working, unless there be results. We must have conversions. As that woman of old said, "Give me children or I die," so is it with the preacher: he must have sinners saved, or he prays to die. Dear hearer, if these times of refreshing may come, our prayer is that you may repent and be converted, that your sins may be blotted out, and so may partake to the full in the priceless blessings of the season.

Once more, the text means, according to the context, the Second Advent. Jesus is yet to come a second time, and like a mighty shower flooding a desert shall his coming be. His Church shall revive and be refreshed; she shall once again lift up her head from her lethargy, and her body from her sepulchre. But woe unto you who are not saved when Christ cometh, for the day of the Lord will be darkness and not light to you. When Christ cometh to the unconverted, "the day shall burn as an oven; and all the proud, yea, and all that do wickedly, shall be stubble." "But who may abide the day of his coming? and who shall stand when he appeareth? for he is like a refiner's fire, and like fullers' soap: and he shall sit as a refiner and purifier of silver: and he shall purify the sons of Levi." Oh, if ye repent and be converted, ye shall stand fully absolved in the day of his coming, when heaven and earth do reel, when the solid rock begins to melt, and the stars, like fig-leaves withered, fall from the tree, when the trumpet sounds exceeding loud and long, "Awake, ye dead and come to judgment," when the grand assize is sitting, and the Judge shall be there—the Judge of quick and dead, to separate the righteous from the wicked. The Lord have mercy upon you in that day; and so he shall if his grace shall make you obedient to the words of our text, "Repent and be converted, that your sins may be blotted out, when times of refreshing shall come from the presence of the Lord."

## 4

## A REVIVAL HARVEST

"Behold, the days come, saith the Lord, that the plowman shall overtake the reaper, and the treader of grapes him that soweth seed; and the mountains shall drop sweet wine, and all the hills shall melt."—Amos 9: 13.

GOD'S promises are not exhausted when they are fulfilled, for when once performed, they stand just as good as they did before, and we may await a second accomplishment of them. Man's promises even at the best, are like a cistern which holds but a temporary supply; but God's promises are as a fountain, never emptied, ever overflowing, so that you may draw from them the whole of that which they apparently contain, and they shall be still as full as ever.

Hence it is that you will frequently find a promise containing both a literal and spiritual meaning. In the literal meaning it has already been fulfilled to the letter; in the spiritual meaning it shall also be accomplished, and not a jot or tittle of it shall fail. This is true of the particular promise which is before us. Originally, as you are aware, the land of Canaan was very fertile; it was a land that flowed with milk and honey.

When, however, the children of Israel thrust in the ploughshare and began to use the divers arts of agriculture, the land became exceedingly fat and fertile, yielding so much corn, that they could export through the Phœnicians both corn, and wine, and oil, even to the pillars of Hercules, so that Palestine became, like Egypt, the granary of the nations. It is somewhat surprising to find that now the land is barren, that its valleys are parched, and that the miserable inhabitants gather miserable harvests from the arid soil. Yet the promise stands true, that one day in the very letter Palestine shall be as rich and fruitful as ever it was.

But while this promise will doubtless be carried out, and every word of it shall be verified, so that the hill-tops of that country shall again bear the vine, and the land shall flow with wine, yet,

I take it, this is more fully a spiritual than a temporal promise; and I think that the beginning of its fulfilment is now to be discerned, and we shall see the Lord's good hand upon us, so that the ploughman shall overtake the reaper, the mountains shall drop sweet wine, and all the hills shall melt.

First, I take the text as being A GREAT PROMISE OF SPIRITUAL REVIVAL. And here, in looking attentively at the text, we shall observe several very pleasant things.

In the first place, we notice a promise of *surprising ingathering.* According to the metaphor here used, the harvest is to be so great that, before the reapers can have fully gathered it in, the ploughman shall begin to plough for the next crop—while the abundance of fruit shall be so surprising that before the treader of grapes can have trodden out all the juice of the vine, the time shall come for sowing seed. One season, by reason of the abundant fertility, shall run into another. Now you all know, beloved, what this means in the Church. It prophesies that in the Church of Christ we shall see the most abundant ingathering of souls. We read of such marvellous revivals a hundred years ago, that the music of their news has not ceased to ring in our ears; but we have seen, alas, a season of lethargy, of soul-poverty among the saints, and of neglect among the ministers of God. Now again God is about to send times of surprising fertility to his Church. When a sermon has been preached in these modern times, if one sinner has been converted by it, we have rejoiced with a suspicious joy; for we have thought it something amazing. But, where we have seen one converted, we may yet see hundreds; where the Word of God has been powerful to scores, it shall be blessed to thousands; and where hundreds in past years have seen it, nations shall be converted to Christ. There is no reason why we should not see all the good that God hath given us multiplied a hundredfold; for there is sufficient vigour in the seed of the Lord to produce a far more plentiful crop than any we have yet gathered. God the Holy Ghost is not stinted in his power. When the sower went forth to sow his seed, some of it fell on good soil, and it brought forth fruit, some twenty fold, some thirty fold, but it is written, "*Some a hundred fold.*" Now, we have been sowing this seed, and thanks be to God, I have seen it bring forth twenty and thirty fold; but I do expect to see it bring forth a hundred fold. I do trust that our harvest shall be so heavy, that while we are taking in the harvest, it shall be time to sow again; that prayer meetings shall be succeeded by the enquiry of souls as to what they shall do to be saved, and ere the enquirers' meeting shall be done, it shall be time again to preach, again to pray; and then, ere that is over, there shall be again another influx of souls, the baptismal pool shall be again stirred, and hundreds of converted men shall flock to Christ.

The promise then, seems to me to convey the idea of surprising ingatherings; and I think there is also the idea of *amazing rapidity*. Notice how quickly the crops succeed each other. Between the harvest and the ploughing there is a season even in our country; in the East it is a longer period. But here you find that no sooner has the reaper ceased his work, or scarce has he ceased it, ere the ploughman follows at his heels. This is a rapidity that is contrary to the course of nature; still it is quite consistent with grace. Among us all there is a tendency to imagine that conversion must be a slow work—that as the snail creeps slowly on its way, so must grace move very leisurely in the heart of man. We have come to believe that there is more true divinity in stagnant pools than in lightning flashes. We cannot believe for a moment in a quick method of travelling to the kingdom of heaven. Every man who goes there must go on crutches and limp all the way; but as for the swift beasts, as for the chariots whose axles are hot with speed, we do not quite understand and comprehend that. Now, mark, here is a promise given of a revival, and when that revival shall be fulfilled this will be one of the signs of it—the marvellous growth in grace of those who are converted. The young convert shall that very day come forward to make a profession of his faith; perhaps before a week has passed over his head you will hear him publicly defending the cause of Christ, and ere many months have gone you shall see him standing up to tell to others what God has done for his soul. There is no need that the pulse of the Church should for ever be so slow. The Lord can quicken her heart, so that her pulse shall throb as rapidly as the pulse of time itself.

A third blessing is very manifest here, and one indeed which is already given to us. Notice the *activity of labour* which is mentioned in the text. God does not promise that there shall be fruitful crops without labour; but here we find mention made of ploughmen, reapers, treaders of grapes, and sowers of seed; and all these persons are girt with singular energy. The ploughman does not wait, because, saith he, the season has not yet come for me to plough, but seeing that God is blessing the land, he has his plough ready, and no sooner is one harvest shouted home than he is ready to plough again. And so with the sower; he has not to prepare his basket and to collect his seed; but while he hears the shouts of the vintage, he is ready to go out to work.

Now one sign of a true revival, and indeed an essential part of it, is the increased activity of God's labourers. I meet with my brethren in the ministry who are able to preach day after day, day after day, and are not half so fatigued as they were; and I saw a brother minister this week who has been having meetings in his church every day, and the people have been so earnest that they will keep him very often from six o'clock in the evening to two in the morning. "Oh!" said one of the members, "our minister will kill himself." "Not he," said I, "that is the kind of work that will kill no man. It is preaching to a sleepy congregation that kills good ministers, but not preaching to earnest people." So when I saw him, his eyes were sparkling, and I said to him, "Brother, you do not look like a man who is being killed." "Killed, my brother," said he, "why I am living twice as much as I did before; I was never so happy, never so hearty, never so well." Said he, "I sometimes lack my rest, and want my sleep, when my people keep me up so late, but it will never hurt me: indeed," he said, "I should like to die of such a disease as that—the disease of being so greatly blessed." There was a specimen before me of the ploughman who overtook the reaper,—of one who sowed seed, who was treading on the heels of the men who were gathering in the vintage. And the like activity we have lived to see in the Church of Christ. Did you ever know so much doing in the Christian world before? There are grey-headed men around me who have known the Church of Christ sixty years, and I think they can bear me witness that they never knew such life, such vigour and activity, as there is at present. Everybody seems to have a mission, and everybody is doing it. There may be a great many sluggards, but they do not come across my path now. I used to be always kicking at them, and always being kicked for doing so. But now there is nothing to kick at—every one is at work—Church of

England, Independents, Methodists, and Baptists—there is not a single squadron that is behindhand; they have all their guns ready, and are standing, shoulder to shoulder, ready to make a tremendous charge against the common enemy. This leads me to hope, since I see the activity of God's ploughmen and vine dressers, that there is a great revival coming,—that God will bless us, and that right early.

We have not yet, however, exhausted our text. The latter part of it says, "The mountains shall drop sweet wine." It is not a likely place for wine upon the mountains. There may be freshets and cataracts leaping down their sides; but who ever saw fountains of red wine streaming from rocks, or gushing out from the hills? Yet here we are told that, "The mountains shall drop sweet wine"; by which we are to understand that conversions shall take place in unusual quarters. This day is this promise literally fulfilled to us. I have this week seen what I never saw before. It has been my lot these last six years to preach to crowded congregations, and to see many, many souls brought to Christ; it has been no unusual thing for us to see the greatest and noblest of the land listening to the word of God; but this week I have seen, I repeat, what mine eyes have never before beheld, used as I am to extraordinary things. I have seen the people of Dublin, without exception, from the highest to the lowest, crowd in to hear the Gospel. I have known that my congregation has been constituted in a considerable measure of Roman Catholics, and I have seen them listening to the Word with as much attention as though they had been Protestants. I have seen men who never heard the Gospel before, military men, whose tastes and habits were not likely to be those of the Puritanic minister, who have nevertheless sat to listen; nay, they have come again; they have submitted to be crowded, that they might press in to hear the Word, and I have never before seen such intense eagerness of the people to listen to the Gospel. I have heard, too, cheering news of work going on in the most unlikely quarters—men who could not speak without larding their conversation richly with oaths—have nevertheless come to hear the Word; they have listened, and have been convinced, and if the impression do not die away, there has been something done for them which they will not forget even in eternity. But the most pleasing thing I have seen is this, and I must tell it to you. Hervey once said, "Each floating ship, a floating hell." Of all classes of men, the sailor has been supposed to be the man least likely to be reached by the Gospel. In crossing over from Holyhead to Dublin and back—two excessively rough passages —I spent the most pleasant hours that I ever spent. The first vessel that I entered, I found my hands very heartily shaken by the sailors. I thought, "What can these sailors know of me?" and they were calling me "*brother*." Of course, I felt that I was their brother too; but I did not know how they came to talk to me in that way. It was not generally the way for sailors to call ministers, brother. There was the most officious attention given, and when I made the enquiry "What makes you so kind?" "Why," said one, "because I love your Master, the Lord Jesus." I enquired, and found that out of the whole crew there were but three unconverted men; that though the most of them had been before without God, and without Christ, yet by a sudden visitation of the Spirit of God they had all been converted. I talked to many of these men, and more spiritual, heavenly minded men I never yet saw. They have a prayer meeting every morning before the boat starts, and another prayer meeting after she comes to port; and on Sundays, when they lay-to off Kingstown or Holyhead, a minister comes on board and preaches the Gospel; the cabins are crowded. Service is held on deck when it can be; and said an eyewitness to me, "The minister preaches very earnestly, but I should like you to hear the men pray; I never heard such praying before," said he, "they pray with such power, as only a sailor can pray." My heart was lifted up with joy, to think of a ship being made a floating Church—a very Bethel for God. When I came back by another ship I did not expect to see the like; but it was precisely the same. The same work had been going on. I walked among them and talked to them. They all knew me. One man took out of his pocket an old leather-covered book in Welsh—"Do you know the likeness of that man in front?" said he. "Yes," I said, "I think I do: do you read these sermons?" "Yes, sir," replied he, "we have had your sermons on board this ship, and I read them aloud as often as I can. If we have a fine passage coming over, I get a few around me, and read them a sermon." Another man told me a story of a gentleman who stood laughing when a hymn was being sung; and one of the men proposed that they should pray for him. They did, and that man was suddenly smitten down, and began on the quay to cry for mercy, and plead with God for pardon. "Ah! Sir," said the sailors, "we have the best proof that there is a God here, for we have seen this crew marvellously brought to a knowledge of the truth; and here we are, joyful and happy men, serving the Lord."

Now, what shall we say of this, but that the mountains drop sweet wine? The men who were loudest with their oaths, are now loudest with their songs; those who were the most darling children of Satan, have become the most earnest advocates of the truth: for mark you, once get sailors converted, and there is no end to the good they can do. Of all men who can preach well, sailors are the best. The sailor has seen the wonders of God in the deep; the hardy British Tar has got a heart that is not made of such cold stuff as many of the hearts of landsmen; and when that heart is once touched, it gives great big beats; it sends great pulses of energy right through his whole frame; and with his zeal and energy what may he not do, God helping him and blessing him?

This seems to be in the text, that a time of revival shall be followed by very extraordinary conversion. But, albeit that in the time of revival, grace is put in extraordinary places, and singular individuals are converted, yet these are not a bit behind the usual converts; for if you notice the text does not say, "the mountains shall drop wine" merely, but they "shall drop *sweet* wine." It does not say that the hills shall send forth little streams; but *all the hills shall melt.* When sinners, profligate and debauched persons, are converted to God, we say, "Well, it is a wonderful thing, but I do not suppose they will be very first-class Christians." The most wonderful thing is, that these are the best Christians alive; that the wine which God brings from the hills is sweet wine; that when the hills do melt they *all* melt. The most extraordinary ministers of any time have been most extraordinary sinners before conversion. We might never have had a John Bunyan, if it had not have been for the profanity of Elstow Green; we might never have heard of a John Newton, if it had not have been for his wickedness on shipboard. I mean he would not have known the depths of Satan, nor the trying experience, nor even the power of divine grace, if he had not been suffered wildly to stray, and then wondrously to be brought back. These great sinners are not a whit behind those who have been trained under pious influences, and so have been brought into the Church. Always in revival you will find this to be the case, that the converts are not inferior to the best of the converts of ordinary seasons—that the Romanist, and the men who have never heard the Gospel, when they are converted, are as true in their faith, as hearty in their love, as accurate in their knowledge, and as zealous in their efforts, as the best of persons who have ever been brought to Christ. "The mountains shall drop sweet wine, and all the hills shall melt."

I must now go on to the other point very briefly—WHAT IS THE DOCTRINAL LESSON WHICH IS TAUGHT IN OUR TEXT: AND WHAT IS TAUGHT TO US BY A REVIVAL? I think it is just this, that God is absolute monarch of the hearts of men. God does not say here *if men are willing*; but he gives an absolute promise of a blessing. As much as to say, "*I* have the key of men's hearts; *I* can induce the ploughman to overtake the reaper; *I* am master of the soil—however hard and rocky it may be *I* can break it, and I can make it fruitful." When God promises to bless his Church and to save sinners, he does not add, "if the sinners be willing to be saved." No, great God! thou leadest free will in sweet captivity, and thy free grace is all triumphant. Man *has* a free will, and God does not violate it; but the free will is sweetly bound with fetters of the divine love till it becomes more free than it ever was before. The Lord, when he means to save sinners, does not stop to ask them whether they mean to be saved, but like a rushing mighty wind the divine influence sweeps away every obstacle; the unwilling heart bends before the potent gale of grace, and sinners that would not yield are made to yield by God. I know this, if the Lord willed it, there is no man so desperately wicked here that he would not be made now to seek for mercy, however infidel he might be; however rooted in his prejudices against the Gospel, Jehovah hath but to will it, and it is done. Into thy dark heart, O thou who hast never seen the light, would the light stream; if he did but say, "Let there be light," there would be light. Thou mayest bend thy fist and lift up thy mouth against Jehovah; but he is thy master yet—thy master to destroy thee, if thou goest on in thy wickedness; but thy master to save thee now, to change thy heart and turn thy will, as he turneth the rivers of water.

If it were not for this doctrine, I wonder where the ministry would be. The power of our preaching is nought—it can do nothing in the conversion of men by itself; men are hardened, obdurate, indifferent; but the power of grace is greater than the power of eloquence or the power of earnestness, and once let that power be put forth, and what can stand against it? Divine Omnipotence is the doctrine of a revival. We may not see it in ordinary days, by reason of the coldness of our hearts; but we *must* see it when these extraordinary works of grace are wrought. Have you never heard the Eastern fables of the dervish, who wished to teach to a young prince the fact of the existence of a God! The fable hath it, that the young prince could not see any proof of the Existence of a First Cause: so the dervish brought a little plant and set it before him, and in his sight that little plant grew up, blossomed, brought forth fruit, and became a towering tree in an hour. The young man lifted up his hands in wonder, and he said, "God must have done this." "Oh, but," said the teacher, "thou sayst, 'God has done this, because it is done in an hour: hath he not done it, when it is accomplished in twenty years?'" It was the same work in both cases; it was only the rapidity that astonished his pupil. So, when we see the Church gradually built up and converted, we lose the sense perhaps of a present God; but when the Lord causes the tree suddenly to grow from a sapling to a strong tall monarch of the forest, then we say, "This is God." We are all blind and stupid in a measure, and we want to see sometimes some of these quick upgoings, these extraordinary motions of divine influence, before we will fully understand God's power. Learn, then, O Church of God today, this great lesson of the nothingness of man, and the Eternal All of God. Learn, disciples of Jesus, to rest on him: look for your success to *his* power, and while you make your efforts, trust not in your efforts, but in the Lord Jehovah. If ye have progressed slowly, give him thanks for progress; but if now he pleases to give you a marvellous increase, multiply your songs, and sing unto him that worketh all things according to the counsel of his will.

I now desire, with great earnestness, as the Holy Ghost shall help me, to make the text A STIMULUS FOR FURTHER EXERTION.

The duty of the Church is not to be measured by her success. It is as much the minister's duty to preach the Gospel in adverse times as in propitious seasons. We are not to think, if God withholds the dew, that we are to withhold the plough. We are not to imagine that, if unfruitful seasons come, we are therefore to cease from sowing our seed. Our business is with act, not with result. The Church has to do her duty, even though that duty should bring her no present reward. "If they hear thee not, Son of man, if they perish they *shall* perish, but their blood will I not require at thine hands." If we sow the seed, and the birds of the air devour it, we have done what we were commanded to do, and the duty is accepted even though the birds devour the seed. We may expect to see a blessed result, but even if it did not come we must not cease from duty. But while this is true so far, it must nevertheless be a divine and holy stimulant to a Gospel labourer, to know that God is making him successful.

And in the present day we have a better prospect of success than we ever had, and we should consequently work the harder. When a tradesman begins business with a little shop at the corner, he waits awhile to see whether he will have any customers. By-and-by his little shop is crowded; he has a name; he finds he is making money. What does he do? He enlarges his premises; the back yard is taken in and covered over; there are extra men employed; still the business increases, but he will not invest all his capital in it till he sees to what extent it will pay. It still increases, and the next house is taken, and perhaps the next; he says, "This is a paying concern, and therefore I will increase it."

I am using commercial maxims, but they are common-sense rules, and I like to talk so. There are, in these days, happy opportunities. There is a noble business to be done for Christ. Where you used to invest a little capital, a little effort, and a little donation, invest more. There never was such heavy interest to be made as now. It shall be paid back in the results cent. per cent.; nay, beyond all that you expected you shall see God's work prospering. If a farmer knew that a bad year was coming, he would perhaps only sow an acre or two; but if some prophet could tell him, "Farmer, there will be such a harvest next year as there never was," he would say, "I will plough up my grass lands, I will stub up those hedges: every inch of ground I will sow." So do you. There is a wondrous harvest coming. Plough up your headlands; root up your hedges; break up your fallow ground, and sow, even amongst the thorns. Ye know not which shall prosper, this or that; but ye may hope that they shall be alike good. Enlarged effort should always follow an increased hope of success.

And let me give you another encouragement. Recollect that even when this revival comes, an instrumentality will still be wanted. The ploughman is wanted, even after the harvest, and the treader of grapes is wanted, however plentiful the vintage; the greater the success the more need of instrumentality. You need not think that if better times should come, the world will do without you. You will be wanted. The ploughman shall never be so much esteemed as when he follows after the reaper, and the sower of seed never so much valued as when he comes at the heels of those that tread the grapes. The glory which God puts upon instrumentality should encourage you to use it.

And now I beseech and intreat you, inhabitants of this great City of London, let not this auspicious gale pass away without singular effort. I sometimes fear lest the winds should blow on us, and we should have our sails all furled, and therefore the good ship should not speed. Up with the canvas now. Oh! put on every stitch of it. Let every effort be used, while God is helping us. Let us be earnest co-workers with him. Methinks I see the clouds floating hither; they have come from the far west, from the shore of America; they have crossed the sea, and the wind has wafted them till the green isle received the showers in its northern extremity. Lo! the clouds are just now passing over Wales, and are refreshing the shires that border on the principality. The rain is falling on Oxfordshire and Gloucestershire; divine grace is distilling, and the clouds are drawing nearer and nearer to us. Mark, they tarry not for men, neither stay they for the sons of men. They are floating o'er our heads today. Shall they float away, and shall we still be left as dry as ever? 'Tis yours today to bring down the rain, though 'tis God's to send the clouds. God has sent this day over this great city a divine cloud of his grace. Now, ye Elijahs, pray it down! To your knees, believers, to your knees. *You* can bring it down, and only you. "For this thing will I be enquired of by the house of Israel to do it for them." "Prove me now herewith," said the Lord of hosts, "and see if I will not open the windows of heaven, and give you such a blessing that you shall not have room to contain it." Will you lose the opportunity, Christians? Will you let men be lost for want of effort? Will you suffer this all-blessed time to roll away unimproved? If so, the Church of one thousand eight hundred and sixty is a craven Church, and is unworthy of its time; and he among you, men and brethren, that has not an earnest heart today, if he be a Christian, is a disgrace to his Christianity. When there are such times as these, if we do not every man of us trust in the plough, we shall indeed deserve the worst barrenness of soul that can possibly fall upon us. I believe that the Church has often been plagued and vexed by her God, because when God has favoured her she has not made a proper use of the favour. "Then," saith he, "I will make thee like Gilboa; on thy mount there shall be no dew; I will bid the clouds that they rain no more rain upon thee, and thou shalt be barren and desolate, till once again I pour out the Spirit from on high."

I have done, when I have uttered a WORD OF WARNING to those of you who know not Christ. I cannot conceive a more doleful wail than that of the man who cries at last in hell, "The harvest is past—*there was a harvest*; the summer is ended—*there was a summer*—and I am not saved." Oh, may my Master smile into your face this day, and say, "I love thy soul; trust me with it. Give up thy sins; turn to me." O Lord Jesus, do it! and men shall not resist thee. Oh! show them thy love, and they must yield. Do it, O thou Crucified One, for thy mercy's sake! Send forth thine Holy Spirit now, and bring the strangers home; and grant thou, O Lord, that many hearts may be fully resigned to thy love, and to thy grace!

## 5

## GO HOME AND TELL OTHERS

"Go home to thy friends and tell them how great things the Lord hath done for thee, and hath had compassion on thee."—Mark 5: 19.

THE case of the man here referred to is a very extraordinary one: it occupies a place among the memorabilia of Christ's life, perhaps as high as anything which is recorded by either of the evangelists. This poor wretch being possessed with a legion of evil spirits had been driven to something worse than madness. He fixed his home among the tombs, where he dwelt by night and day, and was the terror of all those who passed by. The authorities had attempted to curb him; he had been bound with fetters and chains, but in the paroxysms of his madness he had torn the chains in sunder and broken the fetters in pieces. Attempts had been made to reclaim him; but no man could tame him. He was a misery to himself, for he would run upon the mountains by night and day, crying and howling fearfully, cutting himself with the sharp flints, and torturing his poor body in the most frightful manner. Jesus Christ passed by; he said to the devils, "Come out of him." The man was healed in a moment; he fell down at Jesus' feet; he became a rational being—an intelligent man, yea, what is more, a convert to the Saviour. Out of gratitude to his Deliverer, he said, "Lord, I will follow thee whithersoever thou goest; I will be thy constant companion and thy servant; permit me so to be." "No," said Christ, "I esteem your motive; it is one of gratitude to me; but if you would show your gratitude; 'go home to thy friends and tell them how great things the Lord hath done for thee, and hath had compassion on thee.' "

Now, this teaches us a very important fact, namely, this, that true religion does not break in sunder the bonds of family relationship. True religion seldom encroaches upon that sacred, I had almost said divine, institution called *home*; it does not separate men from their families and make them aliens to their flesh and blood. Superstition has done that; an awful superstition, which calls itself Christianity, has sundered men from their kind; but true religion has never done so. Why, if I might be allowed to do such a thing, I would seek out the hermit in his lonely cavern, and I would go to him and say, "Friend, if thou art what thou dost profess to be, a true servant of the living God, and not a hypocrite, as I guess thou art—if thou art a true believer in Christ, and would show forth what he has done for thee, upset that pitcher, eat the last piece of thy bread, leave this dreary cave, wash thy face, untie thy hempen girdle; and if thou wouldst show thy gratitude, go home to thy friends, and tell them what great things the Lord hath done for thee. Canst thou edify the sere leaves of the forest? Can the beasts learn to adore that God whom thy gratitude should strive to honour? Dost thou hope to convert these rocks, and wake the echoes into songs? Nay, go back; dwell with thy friends, reclaim thy kinship with men, and unite again with thy fellows, for this is Christ's approved way of showing gratitude." And I would go to every monastery and every nunnery, and say to the monks, "Come out brethren, come out! If you are what you say you are, servants of God, go home to your friends. No more of this absurd discipline; it is not Christ's rule; you are acting differently from what he would have you; go home to your friends!" And to the sisters of mercy we would say, "Be sisters of mercy to your own sisters; go home to your friends; take care of your aged parents; turn your own houses into convents; do not sit here nursing your pride by a disobedience to Christ's rule, which says, "go home to thy friends." "Go home to thy friends, and tell them how great things the Lord hath done for thee, and had compassion on thee."

*The first sure symptoms of a mind in health*
*Are rest of heart and pleasure found at home.*

True religion cannot be inconsistent with nature. It never can demand that I should abstain from weeping when my friend is dead. "Jesus wept." It cannot deny me the privilege of a smile, when providence looks favourably upon me; for once "Jesus rejoiced in spirit, and said, Father, I thank thee."

It does not make a man say to his father and mother, "I am no longer your son." That is not Christianity, but something worse than what beasts would do, which would lead us to be entirely sundered from our fellows, to walk among them as if we had no kinship with them. To all who think a solitary life must be a life of piety, I would say, "It is the greatest delusion." To all who think that those must be good people who snap the ties of relationship, let us say, "Those are the best who maintain them." Christianity makes a husband a better husband, it makes a wife a better wife than she was before. It does not free me from my duties as a son; it makes me a better son, and my parents better parents. Instead of weakening my love, it gives me fresh reason for my affection; and he whom I loved before as my father, I now love as my brother and co-worker in Christ Jesus, and she whom I reverenced as my mother, I now love as my sister in the covenant of grace, to be mine for ever in the state that is to come. Oh! suppose not, any of you, that Christianity was ever meant to interfere with households; it is intended to cement them, and to make them households which death itself shall never sever, for it binds them up in the bundle of life with the Lord their God, and re-unites the several individuals on the other side of the flood.

"Go home to thy friends, and tell them how great things the Lord hath done for thee, and hath had compassion on thee." First, HERE IS WHAT THEY ARE TO TELL. It is to be a story of *personal experience.* You are not to repair to your houses and forthwith begin to preach. That you are not commanded to do. You are not to begin to take up doctrinal subjects and expatiate on them, and endeavour to bring persons to your peculiar views and sentiments. You are not to go home with sundry doctrines you have lately learned, and try to teach these. At least you are not commanded so to do; you may, if you please, and none shall hinder you; but you are to go home and tell not what you have believed, but what you have *felt*—what you really know to be your own; not what great things you have read, but what great things the Lord hath *done for you.*

Mark this: there is never a more interesting story than that which a man tells about himself. The Rhyme of the Ancient Mariner derives much of its interest because the man who told it was himself the mariner. He sat down, that man whose finger was skinny, like the finger of death, and began to tell that dismal story of the ship at sea in the great calm, when slimy things did crawl with legs over the shiny sea. The Wedding Guest sat still to listen, for the old man was himself a story. There is always a great deal of interest excited by a personal narrative. Virgil, the poet, knew this, and therefore he wisely makes Æneas tell his own story, and makes him begin it by saying, "In which I also had a great part myself." So if you would interest your friends, tell them what you felt yourself. Tell them how you were once a lost abandoned sinner, how the Lord met with you, how you bowed your knees, and poured out your soul before God, and how at last you leaped with joy, for you thought you heard him say within you, "I, even I, am he that blotteth out thy transgressions for my name's sake." Tell your friends a story of your own personal experience.

Note, next, it must be a story of *free grace.* It is not, "Tell thy friends how great things thou hast done thyself," but "how great things *the Lord* hath done for thee." The man who always dwells upon free will and the power of the creature, and denies the doctrines of grace, invariably mixes up a great deal of what he has done himself in telling his experience; but the believer in free grace, who holds the great cardinal truths of the Gospel, ignores this, and declares, "I will tell what the Lord hath done for me. It is true I must tell how I was first made to pray; but I will tell it thus,

*Grace taught my soul to pray,*
*Grace made my eyes o'erflow.*

It is true, I must tell in how many troubles and trials God has been with me; but I will tell it thus,

*'Twas grace which kept me to this day,*
*And will not let me go.*

He says nothing about his own doings, or willings, or prayings, or seekings, but he ascribes it all to the love and grace of the great God who looks on sinners in love and makes them his children, heirs of everlasting life. Go home, young man, and tell the poor sinner's story; go home, young woman, and open your diary, and give your friends stories of grace.

In the next place, this poor man's tale was a *grateful* story. I know it was grateful, because the man said, "I will tell thee how great things the Lord hath done for me"; and (not meaning a pun in the least degree) I may observe, that a man who is grateful is always full of the greatness of the mercy which God has shown him; he always thinks that what God has done for him is immensely good and supremely great. Perhaps when you are telling the story one of your friends will say, "And what of that?" And your answer will be, "It may not be a great thing to you, but it is to me. You say it is little to repent, but I have not found it so; it is a great and precious thing to be brought to know myself to be a sinner, and to confess it." Look them in the face and say, "If you had found him too you would not think it little. You think it little I have lost the burden from my back; but if you had suffered with it, and felt its weight as I have for many a long year, you would think it no little thing to be emancipated and free, through a sight of the Cross." Tell them it is a great story, and if they cannot see its greatness shed great tears, and tell it to them with great earnestness, and I hope they may be brought to believe that you at least are grateful, if they are not. May God grant that you may tell a grateful story. No story is more worth hearing than a tale of gratitude.

And lastly, upon this point: it must be a tale told by a poor sinner who feels himself *not to have deserved* what he has received. "How he hath had *compassion* on thee." It was not a mere act of kindness, but an act of free compassion towards one who was in misery. Oh! I have heard men tell the story of their conversion and of their spiritual life in such a way that my heart hath loathed *them* and their story too, for they have told of their sins as if they did boast in the greatness of their crime, and they have mentioned the love of God not with a tear of gratitude, not with the simple thanksgiving of the really humble heart, but as if they as much exalted themselves as they exalted God. Oh! when we tell the story of our own conversion, I would have it done with deep sorrow, remembering what we used to be, and with great joy and gratitude, remembering how little we deserve these things.

I was once preaching upon conversion and salvation, and I felt within myself, as preachers often do, that it was but dry work to tell this story, and a dull, dull tale it was to me; but on a sudden the thought crossed my mind, "Why, you are a poor lost ruined sinner yourself; tell it, tell it, as you received it; begin to tell of the grace of God as you trust you feel it yourself." Why, then, my eyes began to be fountains of tears; those hearers who had nodded their heads began to brighten up, and they listened, because they were hearing something which the man felt himself, and which they recognised as being true to him, if it was not true to them. "Go home, then, and tell your friends what great things the Lord hath done for you, and how he hath had compassion on you."

But now, in the second place, WHY SHOULD WE TELL THIS STORY? For I hear many of my congregation say, "Sir, I could relate that story to any one sooner than I could to my own friends; I could come to your vestry, and tell you something of what I have tasted and handled of the Word of God; but I could not tell my father, nor my mother, nor my brethren, nor my sisters." Come, then; I will try and argue with you, to induce you to do so, that I may send you home to be missionaries in the localities to which you belong, and to be real preachers, though you are not so by name.

First, for *your Master's sake.* Oh! I know you love him; I am sure you do, if you have proof that he loved you. You can never think of Calvary and his pierced hands and feet, without loving him; and it is a strong argument when I say to you, for his dear sake who loved you so much, go home and tell it. What! do you think we can have so much done for us, and yet not tell it? Our children, if anything should be done for them, do not stay many minutes before they are telling all the company, "such an one hath given me such a present, and bestowed on me such-and-such a favour." And should the children of God be backward in declaring how they were saved when their feet made haste to hell, and how redeeming mercy snatched them as brands from the burning? You love Jesus, young man! I put it to you, then, will you refuse to tell the tale of his love to you? Shall your lips be dumb, when his honour is concerned? Will you not, wherever you go, tell of the God who loved you and died for you? This poor man, we are told, "departed and began to publish in Decapolis how great things Jesus had done for him, and all men did marvel." So with you. If Christ has done much for you, you cannot help it—you must tell it. My esteemed friend, Mr. Oncken, a minister in Germany, told us that so soon as he was converted himself the first impulse of his new-born soul was to do good to others. And where should he do that good? Well, he thought he would go to Germany. It was his own native land, and he thought the command was, "Go home to thy friends and tell them." Well, there was not a single Baptist in all Germany, nor any with whom he could sympathise, for the Lutherans had swerved from the faith of Luther, and gone aside from the truth of God. But he went there and preached, and he has now seventy or eighty Churches established on the continent. What made him do it? Nothing but love for his Master, who had done so much for him, could have forced him to go and tell his kinsmen the marvellous tale of Divine goodness.

But in the next place, are your friends pious? Then go home and tell them, in order *to make their hearts glad*. I received a short epistle written with a trembling hand by one who is past the natural age of man, living in the county of Essex. His son, under God, had been converted by hearing the Word preached, and the good man could not help writing to the minister, thanking *him*, and blessing most of all, his God, that his son had been regenerated. "Sir," he begins, "an old rebel writes to thank you, and above all to thank his God, that his dear son has been converted." I shall treasure up that epistle. It goes on to say, "Go on! and the Lord bless you." And there was another case I heard some time ago, where a young woman went home to her parents, and when her mother saw her, she said, "There! if the minister had made me a present of all London, I should not have thought so much of it as I do of this—to think that you have really become a changed character, and are living in the fear of God."

Now let me tell you a story of Vanderkist, a city missionary, who toils all night long to do good in that great work. There had been a drunken broil in the street; he stepped between the men to part them, and said something to a woman who stood there concerning how dreadful a thing it was that men should thus be intemperate. She walked with him a little way, and he with her, and she began to tell him such a tale of woe and sin too—how she had been lured away from her parents' home in Somersetshire, and had been brought up here in her soul's eternal hurt. He took her home with him and taught her the fear and love of Christ; and what was the first thing she did, when she returned to the paths of godliness and found Christ to be the sinner's Saviour? She said, "Now I must go home to my friends." Her friends were written to; they came to meet her at the station in Bristol, and you can hardly conceive what a happy meeting it was. The father and mother had lost their daughter, they had never heard from her; and there she was brought back and restored to the bosom of her family. Woman! hast thou strayed from thy family? Hast thou left them long? "Go home to thy friends," I beseech thee. Tell mother thou art penitent; tell her that God hath met with thee—that the young minister said, "Go back to thy friends." And if so, I shall not blush to have said these things, though you may think I ought not to have mentioned them; for if I may but win one such soul, I will bless God to all eternity. "Go home to thy friends. Go home and tell them how great things the Lord hath done for thee."

Cannot you imagine the scene, when the poor demoniac mentioned in my text went home? He had been a raving madman; and when he came and knocked at the door, don't you think you see his friends calling to one another in affright, "Oh! there he is again," and the mother running upstairs and locking all the doors, because her son had come back that was raving mad; and the little ones crying because they knew what he had been before—how he cut himself with stones, because he was possessed with devils. And can you picture their joy, when the man said, "Mother! Jesus Christ has healed me; let me in; I am no lunatic now!" And when the father opened the door, he said, "Father! I am not what I was; all the evil spirits are gone; I shall live in the tombs no longer. I want to tell you how the glorious Man who wrought my deliverance accomplished the miracle—how he said to the devils, 'Get ye hence,' and they ran down a steep place into the sea, and I am come home healed and saved." Oh! if such an one, possessed with sin, were here now, and would go home to his friends, to tell them of his release, methinks the scene would be somewhat similar.

I hear one of you say, "Ah! Sir, would to God I could go home to pious friends! But when I go home I go into the worst of places; for my home is amongst those who never knew God themselves and consequently never prayed for me, and never taught me anything concerning heaven." Well, young man, go home to your friends. If they are ever so bad they are your friends. I sometimes meet with young men wishing to join the Church, who say, when I ask them about their father, "Oh, sir, I am parted from my father." Then I say, "Young man, you may just go and see your father before I have anything to do with you; if you are at ill-will with your father and mother I will not receive you into the Church; if they are ever so bad they are *your parents*." Go home to them, and tell them, not to make them glad, for they will very likely be angry with you; but tell them *for their soul's salvation.* I hope, when you are telling the story of what God did for you, that they will be led by the Spirit to desire the same mercy themselves. But I will give you a piece of advice. Do not tell this story to your ungodly friends when they are all together, for they will laugh at you. Take them one by one, when you can get them alone, and begin to tell it to them, and they will hear you seriously. There was once a very pious lady who kept a lodging-house for young men. All the young men were very gay and giddy, and she wanted to say something to them concerning religion. She introduced the subject, and it was passed off immediately with a laugh. She thought within herself, "I have made a mistake." The next morning, after breakfast, when they were all going, she said to one of them, "Sir, I should like to speak with you a moment or two," and taking him aside into another room she talked with him. The next morning she took another, and the next morning another, and it pleased God to bless her simple statement, when it was given individually: but, without doubt, if she had spoken to them altogether, they would have backed each other up in laughing her to scorn. Reprove a man alone. A verse may hit him whom a sermon flies. You may be the means of bringing a man to Christ who has often heard the Word and only laughed at it, but who cannot resist a gentle admonition.

In one of the states of America there was an infidel who was a great despiser of God, a hater of the Sabbath and all religious institutions. What to do with him the ministers did not know.

They met together and prayed for him. But among the rest, one Elder B—— resolved to spend a long time in prayer for the man; after that he got on horseback, and rode down to the man's forge, for he was a blacksmith. He left his horse outside, and said, "Neighbour, I am under very great concern about your soul's salvation; I tell you I pray day and night for your soul's salvation." He left him, and rode home on his horse. The man went inside to his house after a minute or two, and said to one of his faithful friends, "Here's a new argument; here's Elder B—— been down here, he did not dispute, and never said a word to me except this, 'I say, I am under great concern about your soul; I cannot bear you should be lost.' Oh! that fellow," he said, "I cannot answer him"; and the tears began to roll down his cheeks. He went to his wife, and said, "I can't make this out; I never cared about my soul, but here's an elder, that has no connection with me, but I have always laughed at him, and he has come five miles this morning on horseback just to tell me he is under concern about my salvation. After a little while he thought it was time he should be under concern about his salvation too. He went in, shut the door, began to pray, and the next day he was at the deacon's house telling him that he too was under concern about his salvation, and asking him to tell him what he must do to be saved. Oh! that the everlasting God might make use of some of those now present in the same way, that they might be induced to

*Tell to others round*
*What a dear Saviour they have found;*
*To point to his redeeming blood,*
*And say, Behold the way to God!*

There is a third point, upon which we must be very brief. HOW IS THIS STORY TO BE TOLD?

First, *tell it truthfully*. Do not tell more than you know; do not tell John Bunyan's experience, when you ought to tell your own. Do not tell your mother you have felt what only Rutherford felt. Tell her no more than the truth. Tell your experience truthfully; for mayhap one single fly in the pot of ointment will spoil it, and one statement you may make which is not true may ruin it all.

In the next place, *tell it very humbly*. Do not intrude yourselves upon those who are older, and know more; but tell your story humbly; not as a preacher, not *ex-cathedra*, but as a friend and as a son.

Next, *tell it very earnestly*. Let them see you mean it. Do not talk about religion flippantly; you will do no good if you do. Do not make puns on texts; do not quote Scripture by way of joke: if you do, you may talk till you are dumb, you will do no good, if you in the least degree give them occasion to laugh by laughing at holy things yourself.

And then, *tell it very devoutly*. Do not try to tell your tale to man till you have told it first to God. When you are at home let no one see your face till God has seen it. Be up in the morning, wrestle with God; and if your friends are not converted, *wrestle with God for them*; and then you will find it easy work to *wrestle with them for God*. Seek, if you can, to get them one by one, and tell them the story. Do not be afraid; only think of the good you may possibly do. Remember, he that saves a soul from death hath covered a multitude of sins, and he shall have stars in his crown for ever and ever. Let your reliance in the Holy Spirit be entire and honest. Trust not yourself, but fear not to trust him. He can give you words. He can apply those words to their heart, and so enable you to "minister grace to the hearers."

To close up, by a short, and I think, a pleasant turning of the text, to suggest another meaning to it. Very soon with some of us, the Master will say, "Go home to thy friends." You know where the home is. It is up above the stars.

*Where our best friends, our kindred dwell,*
*Where God our Saviour reigns.*

And when we go home to our friends in Paradise, what shall we do? Why, first we will repair to that blest seat where Jesus sits, take off our crown and cast it at his feet, and crown him Lord of all. And when we have done that, what shall be our next employ? Why, we will tell the blessed one in heaven what the Lord hath done for us, and how he hath had compassion on us. And shall such a tale be told in heaven? Yes, it shall be; it has been published there before—blush not to tell it yet again

—for Jesus has told it before. "When he cometh home, he calleth together his friends and neighbours, saying unto them, Rejoice with me, for I have found my sheep which was lost." And thou, poor sheep, when thou shall be gathered in, wilt thou not tell how thy Shepherd sought thee, and how he found thee? Wilt thou not talk with thy brethren and thy sisters, and tell them how God loved thee and brought thee there? You will tell a long story there of God's sustaining, restraining, constraining grace, and I think that when you pause to let another tell his tale, and then another, and then another, you will at last, when you have been in heaven a thousand years, break out and exclaim, "Oh, saints, I have something else to say."

Oh! happy hour! Oh! blessed moment. "Go home," he will soon say, "go home to thy friends, and tell them how great things the Lord hath done for thee, and hath had compassion on thee." Wait awhile; tarry his leisure, and ye shall soon be gathered to the land of the hereafter, to the home of the blessed, where endless felicity shall be thy portion. God grant a blessing for his name's sake.

# 6

## CONTINUE IN PRAYER

"Continue in prayer, and watch the same with thanksgiving."—Col. 4: 2.

HOW greatly do I rejoice that the Churches are aroused to prayer. First, in regard to prayer, the Apostle saith "CONTINUE." Be ye not, O ye intercessors with God for men—be ye not as those whose goodness is as the morning cloud and as the early dew. Do not begin to pray, and then suddenly cease your supplications. That will prove an ignorance as to the the value of the mercy which you seek, and a want of earnestness as to your obtaining it. How many there be who, under a powerful sermon or during a trying providence, have bent their knees suddenly in hasty prayer! They have risen from their knees, and they have forgotten what manner of men they were. Take away the whip from them and they have ceased to run; remove from them the tempest and they have ceased to fly before it. They have ceased to pray when God has ceased to smite. O Church of God! imitate not these heathen men and publicans.

There is a great distinction between the prayer of the real convert and the merely convinced sinner. The merely convicted sinner, terrified by the law, calls but once; the awakened heart, renewed of the Holy Spirit, never ceases to cry until the mercy comes. By the seaside, on the coast of the Isle of Wight, a woman thought she heard, in the midst of the howling tempest, the voice of a man. She listened; it was repeated; she strained her ear again, and she caught, amid the crack of the blast and the thundering of the winds, another cry for help. She ran at once to the beachmen, who launched their boat, and some three poor mariners who were clinging to the mast were saved. Had that cry been but once, and not again, either she might have doubted as to whether she had heard it at all, or else she could have drawn the melancholy conclusion that they had been swept into the watery waste, and that help would have come too late. So when a man prays but once, either we may think that he cries not at all, or else that his desires are swallowed up in the wild waste of his sins, and he himself is sucked down into the vortex of destruction. If the Church of God shall offer prayer, and then shall cease to be in earnest, we shall think her never to have meant her prayers. The exhortation of my text, I think, stands in contrast, then, to the transient prayer which is often offered by ungodly men. *Continue* in prayer; do not pray once and have done with it, but continue in it.

I think further, that the exhortation to continue may be put in opposition to the common dealings of many with God, who pray and pause—are earnest and then cool, earnest and colder still. There is a sharp frost—a rapid thaw, and then a frost again. Their spiritual state is as variable as our own weather; a shower, sunshine, mist, shower, sunshine again. They are everything by turns, and nothing long. There are too many Churches which are just of this character. See them one week, you would believe they would carry all before them, and convert the town or village in which they are located. See them next week, and they are "As sound asleep as a church," which is a common proverb, a church being too often the sleepiest thing in all the world.

Now, I am afraid our Churches have for a considerable period been just in this state; have been sometimes hot and sometimes cold. Look at our revivals everywhere—the American revival, it is a great wave and then dry sand. Look at the Irish revival; I fear that in the end it will come to the same amount. Almost everywhere there have been great stirrings. As if a holy fire had fallen, and was about to burn up all the stubble, all men stand in wonder at it, but it ceases, and a few ashes remain. The fact is, the Church is not healthy; she has intermittent fits of health, she has starts of energy, she has paroxysms of agony; but she does not agonize for souls, she is not always earnest, she is not always busy. Well did Paul need to say to this age as to his own, "*Continue* in prayer," not one week, but every week, not for such a season, but at all seasons. Be ye always crying out unto the Lord your God.

Why? Why should the Church always be in prayer? Understand, we do not mean by this that men ought to leave their business, forsake their shops and neglect their household, to be always supplicating. There were some fanatics in the early Church who gave up everything that they might be always praying; we know what the apostle would have said to them, for did he not say, "If any man will not work, neither let him eat?" There are some lazy people who like praying better than working; let them learn that the Lord accepteth not this at their hands. Did not the Master, even when he was on earth, after he had preached a sermon in Simon Peter's boat—did he not as soon as ever he was done, say to Peter, "Launch out into the deep, and let down your nets for a draught?" to show that work, hard work, the hardest of work is quite in keeping with the hearing and the preaching of the Word; and that no man has any right to forsake his calling to which God has appointed him in his providence, under pretence of seeking the Lord. It is quite possible that you may continue in your labour, and yet continue in prayer. You may not always be in the exercise, but you may always be in the spirit of prayer. If not always shooting the arrow up to heaven, yet always keep the bow well stringed; so shall you always be archers, though not always shooting; so shall you always be men of prayer, though not always in the exercise of praying.

But why should the Church—to come to the question—why should the Church continue in prayer? For several reasons, and the first is, *God will answer her*. It is not possible that God should refuse to hear prayer. It is possible for him to bid the sun stand still, and the moon to stay her monthly march; it is possible for him to bid the waves freeze in the sea, possible for him to quench the light of the stars in eternal darkness, but it is not possible for him to refuse to hear prayer which is based upon his promise and offered in faith. The prayers of God's Church are God's intentions—you will not misunderstand me—what God writes in the book of his decree, which no eye can see, *that* he in process of time writes in the book of Christian hearts where all can see and read. The book of the believer's desire, if those desires be inspired of the Holy Spirit, is just an exact copy of the book of the divine decree. And if the Church be determined today to lift up her heart in prayer for the conversion of men, it is because God determined from before all worlds that men should be converted; your feeble prayer today, believer, can fly to heaven, and awake the echoes of the slumbering decrees of God. Every time you speak to God, your voice resounds beyond the limits of time, the decrees of God speak to your prayer, and cry, "All hail! brother, all hail! thou, too, art a decree!" Prayer is a decree escaped out of the prison of obscurity, and come to life and liberty among men. Pray, brother, pray, for when God inspires you, your prayer is as potent as the decrees of God.

There is a second reason why the Church should continue in prayer, namely, that by her prayers *the world will most certainly be blessed*. In visiting the sick, I saw at the distance, down a long street, the bright light of a fire. In a moment or so the flames seemed to yield; but again it sprang up and lit the heavens, again it became dim, and dimmer still. As we walked along, we said, "They have got the fire under. The engines have been at work, how soon it is out!" I compare this to the Church's work upon the world. The world is as it were wrapped in flames of the fire of sin, and the Church of God must quench those flames. Whenever we meet together and are more earnest in prayer, angels might well see in the distance the flames dimmed and the fire giving way. Whenever we cease our exertions and become languid in our efforts, the flame gets the upper hand of us, and once more spirits from the far-off world can see the fiery mantle surrounding our globe. Hand up your buckets, sirs; every man to the pump; now strip to it every one of you, work while you have life and strength. Now each man to his knee, for it is on our knees that we overcome; each man to his station and to his work, and let us continue to pass from hand to hand the quenching water, till every spark shall be put out, and there shall be a new heaven and a new earth wherein dwelleth righteousness. To stop while but one part of the fabric is on fire, would be to condemn the whole; to pause until the last spark shall be extinct, would be to give up the world to the devouring element. Continue, then, in prayer, till the world be wholly saved, and Christ be universal King.

Thirdly, continue in prayer, because *souls shall be saved as the result of your entreaties*. Can you stand on the beach a moment, —you can scarcely see, but yet you may discern by the lights of lanterns sundry brave men launching the life-boat. It is out —they have taken their seats; helmsman and rowers, all strong hearts, determined to save their fellows or to perish. They have gotten far away now into the midst of the billows and we have lost sight of them, but in spirit we will take our stand in the midst of the boat. What a sea rolled in just then! If she were not built for such weather, she would surely have been overset. See that tremendous wave, and how the boat leaps like a sea-bird over its crest. See now again, it has plunged into a dreary furrow, and the wind, like some great plough, turns up the water on either side as though it were clods of mould. Surely the boat will find her grave, and be buried in the sheet of foam;—but no, she comes out of it, and the dripping men draw a long breath. But the mariners are discouraged, they have strained themselves bending to yonder oars, and they would turn back, for there is small hope of living in such a sea, and it is hardly possible that they will ever reach the wreck. But the brave captain cries out, "Now, my bold lads, for God's sake, send her on! A few more pulls of the oar and we shall be alongside; the poor fellows will be able to hold on a minute or two longer, now pull as for dear life." See how the boat leaps, see how she springs as though she were a living thing, a messenger of mercy intent to save. Again he says, "Once more, once again, and we will do it";—no, she has been dashed aside from the ship for a moment, that sea all but stove her in, but the helmsman turns her round, and the captain cries, "Now, my boys, once more"; and every man pulls with lusty sinews, and the poor shipwrecked ones are saved. Ay, it is just so with us now. Long have Christ's ministers, long have Christ's Church pulled with the Gospel life-boat, let us pull again. Every prayer is a fresh stroke of the oar, and all of you are oarsmen. Pull yet once more, and let us drive the boat ahead, and it may be it will be the last tremendous struggle that shall be required, for sinners shall be saved, and the multitude of the redeemed shall be accomplished. Not we, but grace shall do the work, yet it is ours to be workers for God.

But continue in prayer once more, because prayer is a *great weapon of attack against the error and wickedness of the world.* I see before me the strong bastions of the castle of Sin. I mark the host of men who have surrounded it. They have brought the battering-ram, they have dashed it many times against the gate; it has fallen with tremendous force against it, and you would have supposed that the timbers would be split asunder the first time. But they are staunch and strong; he who made them was a cunning architect, he who depends upon them for his protection is one who knew how to make the gate exceeding massive,—is one who knew the struggle full well which he would have to endure—Prince of Darkness as he is. If he knew of his defeat, yet well he knew how to guard against it if it were possible. But I see this ponderous battering-ram as it has been hurled with giant force again and again upon the gate, and has as often seemed to recoil before the massive bars. Many of the saints of God are ready to say, "Let us withdraw the instrument. Let us take away the besieging armament, we shall never be able to storm this castle, we shall never effect an entrance." Oh, be not craven, sirs, be not craven. The last time the battering-ram thundered in its course, I saw the timbers shake. The very gate did reel, and the posts did rock to and fro; see now they have moved the earth around their sockets. Hell is howling from within because it knows how soon its end must come. Now, Christian warriors, use your battering-rams once more, for the gates begin to shake, and the walls are tottering. They will reel, they will fall ere long,—one more blow, and yet another, and another, and another, and as Israel went up over the walls of Jericho of old, so shall we soon go up over the fallen ruins of the walls of the castle of Sin and Satan. The Church does not know how near her victory is, we do not believe how much God is doing, but let the Holy Spirit for once give us a little more faith, and in confidence that we are nearing the victory, we shall continue in prayer. Turn not back when we have all but overcome, continue still, even till the end shall be, and the voice shall be heard! "Hallelujah, it is done; the kingdoms of this world have become the kingdoms of our Lord and of his Christ."

The second exhortation is WATCH.

Watch, *for you will soon be drowsy if you watch not.* Joshua fought the Amalekites, and I never read that his hand was weary, though the battle occupied a very long day. Moses was on the mountain in prayer, and his hands grew heavy, because prayer is such spiritual work, and we are so un-spiritual that the tendency of prayer upon our nature will be to make us drowsy, unless we watch. It is ill-praying, when we are drowsy. It is ill for a Church that is not half-awake to be in supplication. All eyes must be opened; the judgment, the imagination, the hope, the memory, all must be in full vigour, or else we can scarcely hope that prayer shall be successful. I think I see the Church as I fear she is now. There she is upon her knees, with hands clasped; she mutters a few words; her head droops, for she is weary; again she pleads, and yet again her head is well nigh fallen on her bosom; she is a sleeping Church in prayer. Am I too severe in this my picture? I believe it is true; I think there are some members of the Church thoroughly awake, but they are few. Here, then, we see the value of the exhortation of the apostle—"Continue in prayer and *watch the same.*"

But watch for another reason: because *as soon as ever you begin to pray there will be enemies who will commence the attack.* The Church never was earnest yet without sooner or later discovering that the devil was in earnest too. The devil has had an easy time of it up till the last six or seven years for the Church has been going on her old-fashioned way, doing nothing at all. There was very little abuse of ministers; ministers were getting to be very respectable men, and very little abuse of any section of Christians—they were all getting to be very easy and loveable sort of people. But as sure as the Church, or any section of the Church, shall be right-down in earnest, they will be abused. Never think you are good for anything till the world finds fault with you. Never expect that the world will be friends with the Church. Indeed the world will be friendly enough with the Church, if the Church will not do her duty. Martin Luther used to say, "The world gives me a very bad character, but there is no love lost between us; I can give to it as bad a character as ever it gives to me." Either way we will gratefully accept the honour, and write it down as being a proof of our success.

But watch, O Church of Christ, watch; a struggle awaits thee as sure as ever thou art earnest in prayer. In riding along the south coast of England you may have noticed the old Martello towers in constant succession very near to each other. They are the result of an old scheme of protecting our coast from our ancient enemies. It was supposed that as soon as ever a French ship was seen in the distance the beacon would be fired at the Martello tower, and then, across old England, wherever her sons dwelt, there would flash the fiery signal news that the enemy was at hand, and every man would seize the weapon that was next to him to dash the invader from the shore. Now we need that the Church of Christ should be guarded with Martello towers of sacred watchers, who shall day and night look out for the attack of the enemy. For the enemy will come; if he come not when we are prayerless he will surely come when we are prayerful. If our motto be "Prayer", his watchword will be "Fierce attack." Watch, then, while ye continue in prayer.

But yet again; watch while ye pray *for propitious events which may help you in the answer to your prayer.* I have known sea captains, when they have got their ships loaded with coal, and they have wished to come up to London with their cargo, have been unable to get down the Tyne and out to sea; if they could have got to sea, they could make their passage. And I have once or twice known a wary captain, being well upon the watch, manage to sail out of the river just while there was a little change of the wind, and when his fellows have awakened in the morning, they have missed him from his berth, and he has stolen a march upon them. He watched and they did not, and having lost the wind, they have had to lie in port till he has emptied out his cargo and returned. Now the Church should watch while she prays, to see if she cannot fulfil her own prayers, look out for opportunities of doing good, and see if she cannot steal a march upon her enemies. God doth not always send the Spirit to blow with the same force. We cannot make the wind blow, but we can spread the sails; so, if we cannot command the Spirit of God, when the Spirit of God does come, we can observe his coming and avail ourselves of the glorious opportunity. Watch, then, while ye pray.

Watch, too, *for fresh arguments in prayer.* Heaven's gate is not to be stormed by one weapon but by many. Spare no arrows, Christian. Watch and see that none of the arms in thy armoury are rusty. Besiege the throne of God with a hundred hands, and look at the promise with a hundred eyes. You have a great work on hand for you have to move the arm that moves the world; watch, then, for every means of moving that arm. See to it that you ply every promise; that you use every argument; that you wrestle with all might. When you are wrestling with an antagonist, you must keep your eye on him; you must look to see what he means to do next, or where you can get the next grip at him; see where you can get a hold, or plant your foot, so that you can throw him down. So wrestle with the angel of mercy. Watch while you pray. You cannot wrestle with your eyes shut, nor can you prevail with God unless your own soul be in a watchful state.

One other remark; *watch for the answers to your prayers.* When you post a letter to a friend, requesting a favour, you watch for an answer. When you pray to God for a favour you do not expect him to hear you, some of you. If the Lord were to hear some of your prayers, you would be surprised. I do believe that if God should send to you what you have asked for, you would be quite astonished. Sometimes when I have met with a special answer to prayer and have told it, some have said—"Is it not wonderful!" Not at all; it would be wonderful if it were not so. God says, "Ask, and ye shall receive"; if I should ask and not receive, it would be wonderful. "Seek, and ye shall find"; if you seek and do not find, it is not only wonderful, but I think it is contradictory to God's Word. The Church has but to ask, and she shall receive; she has but to knock, and the door of mercy shall be opened. But we do not believe this. We fritter away God's promises, and clip the edge of them, and then we go to God in prayer, and we think that prayer is a very holy exercise, but we do not think that God really hears us. Too many professors believe it is their duty to pray, but really they are not so enthusiastic as to think that God actually listens, and sends them what they ask for. A man who should say that he knew that God heard his prayers is in some quarters looked upon as an enthusiast. And what is that but a proof that we do not believe this precious Book? For let the most unprejudiced man be a judge, if this Book does not teach that. "Whatsoever we ask in prayer, believing, we shall receive," then it does not teach anything at all; and if it be not true that prayer is a power which prevails with God, then shut this Book; it is not worthy of any confidence, for it does plainly say that which you say it does not mean. The fact is the answers to our prayers are always on the way while we are asking. Sometimes they come while we are yet speaking; sometimes they delay, because we have not prayed as we should. God keeps the mercy back at times, and puts it out at compound interest, because he means to pay it to us interest and all; whereas if we had it at once, we should miss the interest, which sometimes doubles and trebles the principal. We are never losers by his delays, but always gainers. We ought never to say, even though providence should tell us so, that God forgets or is unmindful, we never ought to believe that God has been deaf to our cries, or refused to answer our petitions. A true believer pleading Christ's name and sacrifice, and asking in faith, must and shall receive that which he asks of God.

I am sure that the people of God universally could prove that God does hear prayer. As certainly as ever when you write to a friend you get your answer, more surely and certainly still if you be pleading the name of Christ, God will hear you. But oh! do open your eyes and look out for the blessing. Do watch for it. Be not so simple as to sow the seed and never to look for harvest; do not be planting and never looking for fruit. Give up your prayers, or else expect them to be successful. When we were little children we had a little plot of garden-ground, and we put our seeds into it. I well recollect how the day after I had put in my seed I went and scraped the soil away to see if it was not growing, as I expected it would have been after a day or so at the very longest, and I thought the time amazingly long before the seed would be able to make its appearance above the ground. "That is childish," you would say. I know it is, but I wish you were childish too with regard to your prayers; that you would, when you have put them in the ground, go and see if they have sprung up; and if not at once—be not childish in refusing to wait till the appointed time comes, always go back and see if they have begun to sprout. If you believe in prayer at all, do expect God to hear you. If you do not expect, you will not have it. He will never allow you to think better of him than he is; he will come up to the mark of your thoughts, and according to your faith so shall it be done unto you.

The third point is, GIVE THANKS.

Prayer should be mingled with praise. I have heard that in New England after the Puritans had settled there a long while, they used to have very often a day of humiliation, fasting, and prayer, till they had so many days of fasting, humiliation, and prayer, that at last a good senator proposed that they should change it for once, and have a day of thanksgiving. It is of little use to be always fasting; we ought sometimes to give thanks for mercies received. Why should we go to God as mournful beings, who plead piteously with a hard master who loves not to give? Go not before God with a rueful face, ye people of God, as though he had never heard you before, and you were about to try a great experiment on one who was exceedingly deaf and did not like to give you mercies. God is as pleased to give you his blessing as ever you are to receive it. It is as much to *his* honour as it is to *your* comfort. He takes more pleasure in your prayers than you do in his answers. Come, therefore, boldly, come with thankfulness in your heart and upon your lip, and join the hymn of praise with the cry of prayer. Be thankful for what God has done. "Sing unto him, sing, sing psalms unto him; come into his presence with thanksgivings, and show thyself glad in him with psalms, for the Lord is God and a great King above all gods." So thank him for the past and pray to him for the future. Thank him, too, for the power to pray. Thank him for the privilege of taking the Church's wants before him. And do better still; thank him for the mercy which is to come. Great God I thank thee for the land of China, which shall come unto thee. I praise thee for India, which shall receive thee. I praise thee for Ethiopia, which shall stretch out her arms unto thee. Great God, today we bless thee for what thou wilt do. Thy promise is, in the estimation of our faith, as good as the performance itself. We extol and glorify thee. For thy right hand, O Lord! thy right hand, O Lord, hath dashed in pieces the enemy. Thou hast broken the bow and cut the spear in sunder; thou hast burned the chariot in the fire; thy right hand, O Lord, hath gotten thee the victory. Oh come let us sing unto the Lord, for he hath triumphed gloriously. Let us laud and extol him, for he is King for ever and ever! Say unto Zion, "Thy God reigneth." Behold, he cometh; he cometh to judge the world in righteousness and the people with equity. Rejoice before him, O ye hills, clap your hands, O ye cedars! Let the sea roar and the fulness thereof; the world, and all that dwell therein! Praise him, ye heavens; and ye heaven of heavens; ye spirits that stand before his throne, for he is God, and beside him there is no God. The whole earth praises thee, O God, and all thy creatures bless thee for ever and ever!

Thus with the censor of prayer and praise let us be like priests of God; and thou great High Priest, take thou our sacrifice and offer it before thy Father's face. Put God to the test! See if he do not open the windows of heaven upon you. Be you much in prayer and you shall be much blessed.

## 7

## "A PEOPLE PREPARED FOR THE LORD"

"To make ready a people prepared for the Lord."—Luke 1: 17.

JOHN was the herald of Christ; he was to prepare the way for the coming King, but from this text it appears that he was to do more than that. He was not only to make the road ready for the Lord, but he was also "to make ready a people prepared for the Lord." That was a great work, a task in which he would require strength and wisdom greater than his own. He would need that the Spirit of God, who was to be given without measure to the coming One, should also be in a measure within himself, if he should really "make ready a people prepared for the Lord."

This is not at all a usual expression; at first sight, it hardly looks to us like a Gospel expression. We sang,

*Just as I am—and waiting not*
*To rid my soul of one dark blot,*
*To thee, whose blood can cleanse each spot,*
*O Lamb of God, I come.*

We sang over and over again those words, "Just as I am," "Just as I am," and we are prone to protest against the idea of being prepared for Christ; we preach constantly that no preparation is needed, but that men are to come to Jesus just as they are. Yet here is John the Baptist set apart "to make ready a people prepared for the Lord."

The fact is, that to get men to come to Jesus just as they are, is not an easy thing. To get them to give up the idea of preparing to get them prepared to come without preparing. to get them ready to come just as they are, this is the hardest part of our work, this is our greatest difficulty. If we came and preached to men the necessity of preparation so many weeks of fasting during a long Lent, or through so many days of scourging and penitence, they would attend to us at once, for they would be willing enough to make any preparation of that kind; but, when we say to them, "Come just as you are now, with nothing in your hand to buy the mercy of God, with nothing wherewith to demand or to deserve it," men want a great deal of preparing before they will come to that point. Only the grace of God, working mightily through the Word, by the Spirit, will prepare men to come to Christ thus, prepared by being unprepared so far as any fitness of their own is concerned. The only fit state in which they can come is that of sinking themselves, abandoning all idea of helping Christ, and coming in all their natural impotence and guilt, and taking Christ to be their all in all.

Beloved friends, this is the true preparedness of heart for coming to Christ, the preparedness of coming to him just as you are; and it was John's business thus "to make ready a people prepared for the Lord." That is also my business at this time.

First, *John* made ready "a people prepared for the Lord" BY AROUSING THEIR ATTENTION.

The people were asleep; they had fallen into a condition of religious lethargy, when suddenly there stood in their midst a man clothed with camel's hair, and with a leathern girdle about his loins, a prophet, manifestly, by the boldness and truthfulness of his utterances. He spoke in such a way that the people in general heard of his speaking, and they advertised him by saying the one to the other, "That is a strange man who has begun to preach by the River Jordan, and whose meat is locusts and wild honey."

The whole style of the man set the people wondering and talking; and when they came to listen to him, he did not flatter them, he did not utter more commonplace truths to them, but with burning earnestness he drove straight at their hearts, and spoke like Elijah, the great prophet of fire, had done in the ages gone by. So *he set them thinking*. We have always hope of men when they once begin to think about religion and the things of God. See how the bulk of them hurry on with their eyes tightly shut, rushing fast and yet faster still down to destruction.

You cannot make them stop and think. There are thousands of men who would almost sooner be whipped than be made to think. The last thing to which they will ever come of themselves is thoughtfulness.

Let me appeal to some who are still unconverted. Did you ever give the affairs of your soul the benefit of an hour's serious consideration? You have your regular time for stock-taking, those of you who are in business; do you ever take stock of your spiritual estate? I know that you are not such fools as to neglect your ledgers, you cast up your accounts to see whereabouts you are financially; but do you cast up the account between God and your own soul, and look the matter fairly and squarely in the face? Oh, if we could but bring you to do this, we should feel that you were being prepared for coming to Christ just as you are, for no man will come to Christ while he is utterly careless and thoughtless! Faith is a matter of thought; it requires a mind aroused from slumber, a mind that has taken wing; and John the Baptist did good service for his Master when he startled men into that condition, and so made them consider their ways.

He did more than that, for, having first made them think, *he preached to them a Saviour.* He told them that One was coming with power to baptize them after a higher sort than his baptism. He cried, "Behold the Lamb of God, which taketh away the sin of the world," and this message infused into the people a measure of hope. The poor people said, "What shall we do?" for they had a hope that there was something to be gained. Even the tax-gatherers, despised as they were, began to look up, and think that there might be something even for them, so they said to John, "Master, what shall we do?" And the rough Roman soldiers thought, "There may be something for us," so they also asked, "And what shall we do?" John inspired the multitudes with hope.

It is a very blessed state of mind for a man to get in when he begins to hope that he may be saved. Then he will be prepared to come to Jesus, just as he is, when he feels that he is not shut up to despair. "Oh!" says the poor man, "I need not, after all be lost; I need not abide for ever under the wrath of God. There is an open door set before me, there is a way of mercy even for me." I wish it were possible that everybody whom

I am now addressing had that feeling; it would be part of the making ready of "a people prepared for the Lord" when thought had blossomed into hope.

But John led his hearers on further than that, for *they began to expect something as well as to hope for it.* They epected that the Christ would speedily come, and they expected some great blessings through the coming of the Messiah. And oh! when men, after hearing the gospel, have great expectations concerning God and his salvation, surely their expectations will not be long disappointed. I remember a man coming one day to see me, and he said that he wished to take a sitting in the Tabernacle. He had been hearing me for some time, and he wanted to take a seat; but he desired to be very honest with me, and not to take a seat except upon a right understanding. I asked, "What is the difficulty, my friend?" "Well," he replied, "the person who sat next to me on Sunday told me that, if I became a regular hearer here, you would expect me to be converted." "Well," I answered, "that is true, I shall expect it." "But," said he, "you do not mean that you will require it of me." "Oh, dear no!" I replied, "nothing of the sort; I do not expect you to convert yourself; but I hope and trust that you will be converted, that is what I mean. I shall expect that God, in his grace, will meet with you and save you." "Oh!" he said, "I hope that, too; only I mean that I could not guarantee it." "Ah!" I said, "I see that you have taken the word 'expect' in the wrong sense; but I think, dear friend, that if you come expecting to be converted, and I preach expecting that you will be converted, it is highly probable that it will soon take place." "Oh!" he exclaimed, "God grant it!" A very few weeks after our conversation, he came and told me that the expectation in which we had united had been fulfilled, and he trusted that he had found the Saviour. When people come really expecting a blessing, they will be sure to get it. I do believe that some folk go to hear ministers with the idea that there will be something to find fault with, and, of course, they find that it is so; and when people come to hear another preacher, with the hope and expectation that God will bless them, of course God does bless them. Their expectation is divinely fulfilled. I have always a bright hope that a man will lay hold on Christ when he begins to expect to be saved, for he feels then that the time has come for him to find eternal life.

John did more than this, for he cried, "Repent ye: for the kingdom of heaven is at hand." that is to say, *he put a pressure of presentness upon the people.* A brother, who is an eminent preacher, but who uses rather long words, was explaining to me the benefit of the preaching of Mr. Fullerton and Mr. Smith in his place of worship. He said, "I do not know exactly why these brethren were the means of the conversion of many in my place whom I had never reached, but I perceived that they had the power to precipitate decision." It sounded rather strange, but when I thought it over a little while, I rather liked the expression, "the power to precipitate decision." That is the power that leads men to make up their minds, and say "Yes," or "No," to feel that the decision has to be made at once, and that the putting of it off is impossible because it would be a kind of insanity. Now that is the meaning of what John said, "The kingdom of heaven is at hand! Repent ye! He is coming who wields the axe of the divine justice; bear fruit, or else be cut down. He is coming who uses the great winnowing fan; be the true wheat, or else be blown away." He put the truth so pointedly, and so earnestly, that he did by that means make ready "a people prepared for the Lord."

Now, secondly, John made the people ready for Christ BY AWAKENING THEIR CONSCIENCES.

His very first utterance, as I have reminded you, was, "Repent ye, for the kingdom of heaven is at hand." "Repent! Repent! Repent!" was John's continual cry. This awakened the consciences of his hearers concerning *their sin.* Preaching repentance meant, "You have sinned; change your mind in reference to that sin. You have sinned; quit the sin, mourn over it, ask forgiveness for it. Repent ye!" Whenever a man brings to the minds of others their sins, when he so does it that they begin to feel that they have sinned, then they are being prepared for the Lord, for no man will come to the Saviour unless he knows that he needs a Saviour; and no man will feel that he needs a Saviour until he feels that he is a sinner. Hence it is a real preparation of men for Christ to convince them of sin.

This John did; he brought their sin before them, and then *he showed them their need of cleansing*, for he stood by the River Jordan, not with a scallop shell, as some depict him, but he stood by the flowing stream, ready to immerse all those who repented. This was practically saying to them, "You need to be washed, you need to be cleansed; and I show you this truth as I baptize you with water unto repentance. As your bodies are washed with pure water, so must your souls be washed and made clean ere you can enter heaven." This was John's plain teaching by his action as well as by his words.

Then he went straight away to arousing their consciences by telling them of *their need of a change of life*. He said that it was no use for them to pretend to grieve over the past, and then continue to sin in the same fashion. "Bring forth fruits," said he, "meet for repentance," or, "answerable to amendment of life," as the margin has it. And he took pains to point out what the fruits must be. If they were men of greed, they must become generous, and give to their needy neighbours. If they had been unrighteous and exacting, they must become honest. If they had been domineering, and brutal, and murmuring, they must become contented and quiet and gentle.

He not only preached to the multitudes about repentance of sin in general, but *he pointed out the precise sin of each class of persons* that came to him, and urged them to perform the special duties which they had neglected. Now I believe, as I have often said, that there is no sewing with silk thread alone; you must have a needle as well. You need a sharp needle to go first to draw the thread through the material; so you must preach the law, you must denounce sin, and you must individualize, and condemn special sins; and you must be personal, and pointed, or else men will not feel in their consciences what you say to them. Conscience is very apt to get seared as with a hot iron, to lose sensitiveness, so as to be no use at all as a conscience. Some say that conscience is a spark of deity, a divine monitor; it is nothing of the sort, in many a man it is almost extinct, for it does not act at all. The preacher who would "make ready a people prepared for the Lord" must come out with his axe, and lay it to the root of the trees; he must be definite and distinct in indicating this sin and that sin, and crying to all men, "Repent of these sins. Give them up. Get clear from them. Be washed from them; or else, as

God lives, when the Christ himself comes, it will not be to save you, but to blow you away with his winnowing fan as the chaff is blown into the fire."

Thirdly, John had "to make ready a people prepared for the Lord" BY POINTING OUT THE NATURE OF TRUE RELIGION.

He showed that *it did not depend upon external privileges*. As soon as ever John began to preach, the men of Jewish race, proud of their pedigree, pressed near; and John, with all the courage that a servant of the Lord could have, said, "Begin not to say within yourselves, We have Abraham to our father: for I say unto you, That God is able of these stones to raise up children unto Abraham." You see the drift of his preaching do you not? He says, practically, "Men and women, there is no virtue in your boasted privileges, there is no merit in your religious descent. As for supposing yourselves to be the peculiar people of God, you are not to be saved that way. Say not, We have Abraham to our father." Oh, how many hug that idea, "My father was a Christian." Others say, "Well, I live in a Christian country." They suppose that there is something in the very race from which they have sprung. Away with all such notions, for whatever external privileges you may have had, they are not sufficient to secure salvation for you.

Then came the Pharisees and the Sadducees; they were the religious people of the time, the great observers of all outward propriety, but John taught them that *true religion is not the same as official pretension*. He called them a "generation of vipers." This was very disrespectful, and very shocking indeed on his part; all the newspapers of the period, if there had been any, would have cried him down for his want of charity, but he wanted those who came to him to understand that true religion was not the same as professing to be religious. It was not making broad the borders of their garments, it was not wearing a text of Scripture as a phylactery between their eyes, it was not making long prayers at the corners of the streets, that would save them; there must be a thorough change of heart. So John spoke straight out; and this, I believe, is a great way of preparing men for coming to Christ, when you tell them, "It is not your early training, it is not your going to church or chapel, it is not your infant sprinkling and your confirmation, it is not even your adult baptism, nor your saying prayers and reading the Bible, that will save you; but 'ye must be born again.' There must be an inward spiritual change, wrought by the Holy Spirit. You must believe in Jesus Christ, whom God has sent, and you must so believe in him as to be made new creatures in him, or else you cannot be saved." Now, when men realize that all this is true, it startles them out of their false refuges, and makes them ready to flee to the only true refuge, so that it is really the way of making ready "a people prepared for the Lord."

While John set forth this matter negatively, putting down all the wrong hopes of his hearers, he was exceedingly plain in telling them that the way of salvation would involve them in *the necessity of being right before God*. "There," said he, "the proof of a tree's life is its fruit, and the evidence of your new life will be your good works. 'Now also the axe is laid unto the root of the trees; therefore, every tree which bringeth not forth good fruit is hewn down, and cast into the fire.'" Unless our religion makes us holy, it has not done anything for us that is really worth doing. Unless we hate sin, and love righteousness, our religion is a sham and a lie. John stated that truth very plainly; and that is the way to drive men to Christ.

He told them also that the trial of a life would be by its weight as well as by its fruit. "Look," said he, "at the heap that lies on the threshing-floor. He that hath the fan in his hand begins to winnow it; that which is light and chaffy is blown away, that which has wheat in it remains on the floor. So," said he, "there must be weight about your religion—stability, reality, sincerity. There must be heart-work in it, it must be no pretence; it must be true from beginning to end, or else it shall no more avail you than a heap of chaff would avail the husbandman when it is blown into the fire."

Then John taught his hearers that Christ himself would be the great Trier of human hearts; not ministers or fellow-professors, but Christ himself. When men feel this to be true, then they begin to say to themselves, "There is more required than we at present possess. There is more demanded than we can ever manufacture of ourselves. Let us go to him that hath it, and ask him for it. Let us go to Christ, who hath grace to bestow upon the poor and needy."

*Not the labours of my hands*
*Can fulfil thy law's demands:*
*Could my zeal no respite know,*
*Could my tears for ever flow,*
*All for sin could not atone*
*Thou must save and thou alone.*

Now I shall close my discourse by noticing a fourth way in which John made ready "a people prepared for the Lord." He did it BY DECLARING THE GRACE AND POWER OF JESUS CHRIST.

If I were to preach to you merely to arouse your attention, to awaken your consciences to a sense of sin, or simply to show you the nature of true religion, yet you would not be prepared for Christ unless also you knew something about him, something about his suitableness and his power to save you. So, *John preached Jesus Christ as a mighty and glorious Saviour on whom the Spirit rested.* He says that, when he baptized our Lord, as Jesus came up out of the water, "I saw the Spirit descending from heaven like a dove, and it abode upon him. And I knew him not: but he that sent me to baptize with water, the same said unto me, Upon whom thou shalt see the Spirit descending, and remaining on him, the same is he which baptizeth with the Holy Ghost." John boldly preached, and told the people that the Spirit of God rested upon Jesus Christ, yea, abode upon him. Now, this would lead them to him, and this should lead you to him. If you want the grace of penitence, Christ has it to give you. If you want the grace of supplication, he has it to give you. If you want the grace of faith, he has it. If you want the grace of holiness, he has it. "It pleased the Father that in him should all fulness dwell," "and of his fulness have all we received, and grace for grace." John taught this to his hearers, and I teach it to you. If you are willing to have it, it is freely presented to you. He who makes you willing to receive is certainly willing to give. If he has emptied you, and prepared you to receive of his fulness, do not think that he will refuse you when you come to him for it. He hath said, "Him that cometh to me I will in no wise cast out." All thy requirements are fully met in him. The Spirit of God dwells in him as a fulness, and as an abiding fulness; therefore, do but believe in him, and even that faith he will give thee, do but trust him, and thou art saved, and fully supplied in him who can meet all the necessities of thy case.

John also told his hearers that *the Christ whom he preached was able to baptize them with the Holy Ghost.* "See," says he, "I only plunge you in the flowing stream, I can do nothing more for you than dip you in this River Jordan, on profession of your repentance of sin; but this Saviour, this Christ of God, can immerse you into the Spirit of God. He can give you of his power to fill you; you can be baptized into the Holy Ghost by him." Dost thou hear this? Jesus Christ can come and give thee the Holy Spirit in such measure that thou shalt be baptized into him

*Plunged in the Godhead's deepest sea,*
*And lost in his immensity.*

This will make thee to be really his, and make thee truly to live unto him. The very fulness of grace, then, is with Christ, and he is prepared to give it; and this should make men prepared to receive it. Did not the poor prodigal son say of the provision in his father's house, "There is bread enough and to spare"? It was partly that which made him go to his father's house; and we may say of the Spirit who is in Christ, "There is enough and to spare for every poor sinner who comes to him;" therefore, come along with thee, be prepared at once to come and receive the Saviour.

Lastly, John said in his preaching, "Behold the Lamb of God, which taketh away the sin of the world." *He pointed out Christ as the Sin-bearer,* bearing human guilt in his own person. That is the master-key which lets men into the kingdom of heaven. Oh! how I do delight to preach Christ as the Substitute Christ as the atoning sacrifice; and when you have heard Christ preached in that way, it makes you ready, "a people prepared for the Lord." How can men come to Christ if they do not know what Christ has done for them? If you do not understand that he suffered in your stead, the Just for the unjust, to bring you to God, how can you come to Christ? But when you have learned that holy and blessed doctrine of Christ's propitiation for human sin, why, then, methinks, you will leap at the very sound of it, and say, "Yes, I will take this propitiation to be a sacrifice for me. Blessed Lamb of God,

*My faith would lay her hand*
*On that dear head of thine,*
*While like a penitent I stand*
*And there confess my sin.*

John's preaching Christ was the best way of making ready "a people prepared for the Lord," and there is no better way of preparing you to come to Jesus. Oh, that God would grant to some of you that "precipitation of decision" of which my learned friend spoke! Oh, that in some lives the turning-point might be reached now, the happy moment when they should decide for Christ! Lord, decide them! My friend, you have come to the cross-roads; peradventure, today, if you reject the Saviour, it will be your last rejection of him, and it will finally seal your doom; and I am sure, with no peradventure whatever, that if this day you look to Jesus, and trust to his finished work, you shall be saved, and saved for ever.

# 8

## WITHOUT CHRIST—NOTHING

"Without me ye can do nothing."—John 15: 5.

THIS is not the language of a man of ordinary mould. No saint, no prophet, no apostle would ever have addressed a company of faithful men, and have said to them, "without me ye can do nothing." Had Jesus Christ been, as some say, a good man, and nothing more, such language as this would have been unseemly and inconsistent. Among the virtues of a perfect man we must certainly reckon modesty, but this from a mere man would have been shamelessly immodest. It is impossible to conceive that Jesus of Nazareth, had he not been more than man, could ever have uttered the sentence, "Without me ye can do nothing." I hear in this sentence the voice of that Divine Person without whom was not anything made that was made. The majesty of the words reveals the Godhead of him that uttered them. The "I am" comes out in the personal word "me," and the claim of all power unveils the Omnipotent. These words mean Godhead or nothing. The spirit in which we listen to this language is that of adoration. Let us bow our heads in solemn worship, and so unite with the multitude before the throne who ascribe power and dominion and might to him that sitteth upon the throne and to the Lamb.

In this adoring state of mind we shall be the better prepared to enter into the innermost soul of the text. I am not going to preach upon the moral inability of the unregenerate, although in that doctrine I most firmly believe; for that truth did not come in our Lord's way when he uttered these words, neither did he allude to it. It is quite true that unregenerate men, being without Christ, can do no spiritual action whatever, and can do nothing which is acceptable in the sight of God; but our Lord was not speaking to unregenerate men at all, nor speaking about them. He was surrounded by his apostles, the eleven out of whom

Judas had been weeded, and it is to them as branches of the true vine that he says, "Without me ye can do nothing." The statement refers to such as are in the wine, and even to such as have been pruned, and have for a while been found abiding in the stem, which is Christ; even in such there is an utter incapacity for holy produce if separated from Christ.

We are not called upon just now to speak upon all forms of doing, as beyond us, but of that form of it which is intended in the text. There are certain forms of doing in which men excel who know little or nothing of Christ; but the text must be viewed in its own connection, and the truth is clear. Believers are here described under the figure of branches in the vine, and the doing alluded to must therefore be the bearing of fruit. I might render it, "Apart from me ye can produce nothing—make nothing, create nothing, bring forth nothing." The reference, therefore, is to that doing which may be set forth by the fruit of the vine branch, and therefore to those good works and graces of the Spirit which are expected from men who are spiritually united to Christ: it is of these that he says, "Without me ye can do nothing." Our text is only another form of the fourth verse: "As the branch cannot bear fruit of itself, except it abide in the vine; no more can ye except ye abide in me." I am therefore going to address myself to you who profess to know and love the Lord, and are anxious to glorify his name, and I have to remind you that union to Christ is essential; for only as you are one with him, and continue to be so, can you bring forth the fruits which prove you to be truly his.

Reading again this solemn sentence, "Without me ye can do nothing," it first of all excites in me AN ASPIRATION OF HOPE. There is something to be *done*, our religion is to have a grand practical outcome. I have been thinking of Christ as the vine, and of the myriads of branches in him, and my heart has hoped for great things. From such a root what a vintage must come! Being branches in him, what fruit we must produce! There can be nothing scanty or poverty-stricken in the fruitage of a vine so full of sap. Fruit of the best quality, fruit in the utmost abundance, fruit unrivalled, must be borne by such a vine. That word "*do*" has music in it. Yes, Jesus went about doing good, and, being in him, we shall do good. Everything about him is efficient, practical,—in a word, fruitbearing; and being joined to him much will yet be done by us. We have been saved by the almighty grace of God apart from all doings of our own, and now that we are saved we long to *do* something in return: we feel a high ambition to be of some use and service to our great Lord and Master. The text, even though there be a negative in it, yet raises in our soul the hope that ere we go hence and be no more we may even here on earth do something for Christ.

Beloved, there is the ambition and hope before us of doing something in the way of glorifying God by bringing forth *the fruits of holiness, peace, and love.* We would adorn the doctrine of God our Saviour in all things. By pureness, by knowledge, by longsuffering, by love unfeigned, by every good and holy work we would show forth the praises of our God. Apart from the Lord Jesus we know we cannot be holy; but joined unto him we overcome the world, the flesh, and the devil, and walk with garments unspotted from the world. The fruit of the Spirit is love, joy, peace, longsuffering, gentleness, goodness, faith, meekness, temperance, and all manner of holy conversation. For none of these things are we equal in and of ourselves, and yet by faith we say with Paul, "I can do all things through Christ which strengtheneth me." We may be adorned with plentiful clusters, we may cause the Saviour to have joy in us that our joy may be full: great possibilities are before us.

We aspire not only to produce fruit in ourselves, but to bear much *fruit in the conversion of others*, even as Paul desired concerning the Romans, that he might have fruit among them. In this matter we can do nothing whatever alone; but being united unto Christ we bring forth increase unto the Lord. Our Lord Jesus said, "The works that I do shall ye do also, and greater works than these shall ye do, because I go unto the Father." A hope springs up in our bosom that we may each one of us bring many souls to Jesus. Not because we have any power in ourselves, but because we are united to Jesus we joyfully hope to bring forth fruit in the way of leading others to the knowledge of the Gospel.

My soul takes fire of hope, and I say to myself, If it be so, all these branches, and all alive, how much *fruit of further blessing* will ripen for this poor world. Men shall be blessed in us because we are blessed in Christ. What must be the influence of ten thousand godly examples! What must be the influence upon our country of thousands of Christian men and women practically advancing love, peace, justice, virtue, holiness! And if each one is seeking to bring others to Christ what numerous conversions there must be, and how largely must the church of God be increased. Do you not know that if there were only ten thousand real Christians in the world, yet if each one of these brought one other to Christ every year it would not need twenty years to accomplish the conversion of the entire population of the globe? This is a simple sum in arithmetic which any schoolboy can work out. I sit me down and dream right comfortably, according to the promise, "Your young men shall see visions, and your old men shall dream dreams." See these thousands of branches, proceeding from such a stem as Christ Jesus, and with such sap as the Holy Ghost flowing through them; why, surely, this vine must soon clothe the mountains with its verdure, and there shall not remain a single barren rock unadorned with the blessed foliage! Then shall the mountains drop sweet wine, and all the hills shall melt. Not because of any natural fertility in the branches, but because of their glorious root, and stem, and sap, each one shall bear full clusters, and each fruitful bough shall run over the wall. Beloved friends in Christ, have you not strong desires to see some such consummation? Do you not long to take a share in the high enterprise of winning the world to Christ? Oh, ye that are young and full of spirits, do you not long to press to the front of this great crusade? Our souls pine to see the knowledge of the Lord covering the earth as the waters cover the sea. It is glad tidings to us that, joined unto Christ, we can do something in this great business, something upon which the Lord will smile, something which shall redound to the glory of his name. We are not condemned to inaction; we are not denied the joy of service, the superior blessedness of giving and of doing: the Lord hath chosen us and ordained us to go and bring forth fruit, fruit that shall remain. This is the aspiration which rises in our soul; the Lord grant that we may see it take actual form in our lives.

But now, in the second place, there passes through my heart a shudder, A SHUDDER OF FEAR. Albeit I glow and burn with strong desire and rise upon the wing of a mighty ambition to do something great for Christ, yet I read the text, and a sudden trembling takes hold upon me. "Without me"; it is possible, then, that I may be without Christ, and so may be utterly incapacitated for all good. Come, friends, I want you to feel, even though it cast a cold chill over you, that you may possibly be "without Christ". You profess to be in Christ; but are you so? The large majority of those to whom I speak are visible members of the visible church of Christ; but what if you should *not be so in him as to bring forth fruit?* Evidently there are branches which in a certain sense are in the vine, and yet bring forth no fruit! It is written, "Every branch in me that beareth not fruit he taketh away." Yes, you are a member, perhaps an elder, perhaps a deacon, possibly a minister, and so you are in the vine; but are you bringing forth the fruits of holiness? Are you consecrated? Are you endeavouring to bring others to Jesus Christ? Or is your profession a thing apart from a holy life, and devoid of all influence upon others? Does it give you a name among the people of God and nothing more? Say, is it a mere natural association with the church, or is it a living, supernatural union with Christ? Let the thought go through you and prostrate you before him who looks down from heaven upon you, and lifts his pierced hand, and cries, "Without me ye can do nothing." If you are without Christ, what is the use of carrying on that Bible Class, for you can do nothing? What is the use of my coming to this pulpit if I am without Christ? What is the use of your going down into the Sunday School this afternoon if, after all, you are without Christ? Unless we have the Lord Jesus ourselves we cannot take him to others. Unless within us we have the living water springing up unto eternal life, we cannot overflow so that out of our midst shall flow rivers of living water.

I will put the thought another way; what if you should be in Christ, and *not so in him as to abide in him?* It appears from our Lord's words that some branches in him are cast forth and are withered. "If a man abide not in me, he is cast forth as a branch, and is withered." Some who are called by his name, and reckoned among his disciples, whose names are heard whenever the muster-roll of the church is read, yet do not continue in him. What if it should happen that you are only in Christ on a Sunday, but in the world all the week! What if you are only in Christ at the communion table, or at the Prayer Meeting, or at certain periods of devotion? What if you are off and on with Christ! What if you play fast and loose with the Lord! What if you are an outside saint and an inside devil! And yet some persist in attempting to hold an intermittent communion with Christ. This will not do. We must be so in Christ as to be always in him, or else we are not living branches of the living vine, and we cannot produce fruit. If there were such a thing as a vine branch that was only occasionally joined to the stem, would you expect it to yield a cluster to the husbandman? So neither can you if you are off and on with Christ. You can do nothing if there be not constant union.

One year when I was travelling towards my usual winter resting-place I halted at Marseilles, and there was overtaken by great pain. In my room in the hotel I found it cold, and so I asked for a fire. I was sitting in a very desponding mood, when suddenly the tears came to my eyes, as if smitten with a great sorrow. I shall never forget the thoughts which stirred my heart. The porter came in to light the fire. He had in his hand a bundle of twigs. I called to him to let me look at it. He was about to push it into the stove as fuel with which to kindle the fire. As I took the bundle into my hand, I found it was made of vine branches that had been cut off now that the pruning time was come. Ah me, I thought, will this be my portion? Here I am, away from home, unable to bear fruit, as I love to do. Shall I end with this as my portion? Shall I be gathered for the fire? Those vine shoots were parts of a good vine, no doubt—branches that once looked fair and green; but now they were fuel for the flame. They had been cut off and cast off as useless things, and then men gathered them and tied them in bundles, and they were ignobly thrust into the fire. What a picture!

"Men gather them, and cast them into the fire, and they are burned." Shall this be the lot of any of us who have named the name of Christ? Well did I say a shudder may go through us as we listen to those words, "without me." Our end without Christ will be terrible indeed. First, no fruit; then no life; and at last no place among the saints, no existence in the church of God. Without Christ we do nothing, we are nothing, we are worse than nothing. Here is grave cause for heart-searching, and I leave the matter with you to that end.

Having come so far in our second head, under the third I behold A VISION OF TOTAL FAILURE. "Without me," says the text, "ye can do nothing"—ye can produce nothing. The visible Church of Christ has tried this experiment a great many times already, and always with the same result. Separated from Christ, his church can do nothing which she was formed to do. She is sent into the world upon a high enterprise, with noble aims before her, and grand forces at her disposal; but if she could cease from communion with Christ she would become wholly incapable.

Now what are the outward signs of any community being apart from Christ? Answer, first, It may be seen in *a ministry without Christ in its doctrine.* This we have seen ourselves. Woe worth the day that it is so! History tells us that not only in the Romish church and the Anglican church, but among the Nonconformist churches, Christ has been at times forgotten. Not only among Unitarians, but among Presbyterians, Methodists, Baptists, all round, Jesus has been dishonoured. Attempts have been made to do something without Christ as the truth to be preached. What folly it is! They preach up intellectualism, and hope that this will be the great power of God; but it is not. "Surely," say they, "novelties of thought and refinements of speech will attract and win! The preachers aspire to be leaders of thought; will they not command the multitude and charm the intelligent? Add music and architecture, and what is to hinder success?" Many a young minister has given up his whole mind to this—to try and be exceedingly refined and intellectual; and what has he done with these showy means? The sum total is expressed in the text—"Nothing": "Without me ye can do nothing." What emptiness this folly has created: when the pulpit is without Christ the pews are soon without people. I knew a chapel where an eminent divine was to be heard for years. A converted Jew coming to London to visit a friend, set out on Sunday morning to find a place of Christian worship, and he chanced to enter the chapel of this eminent divine. When he came back he said, that he feared he had made a mistake; he had turned into a building which he hoped was a Christian place of assembly; but as he had not heard the name of Jesus all the morning, he thought perhaps he had fallen in with some other religionists. I fear that many modern sermons might just as fairly have been delivered in a Mahometan mosque as in a Christian church. We have too many preachers of whom we might complain, "they have taken away my Lord, and I know not where they have laid him." Christianity without Christ is a strange thing indeed. A sermon without Christ as its beginning, middle, and end is a mistake in conception and a crime in execution. However grand the language it will be merely much-ado-about-nothing if Christ be not there.

Further, without acknowledging always *the absolute supremacy of Christ* we shall do nothing. Jesus is much complimented nowadays; but he is not submitted to as absolute Lord. I hear many pretty things about Christ from men who reject his Gospel. "Lives of Christ" we have in any quantity. Oh for one which would set him forth in his glory as God, as Head of the church and Lord of all. I should greatly like to see a "Life of Christ" written by one who knew him by communion with him and by reverently sitting at his feet. Most of the pretty things about Jesus which I read nowadays seem to have been written by persons who have seen him through a telescope at a great distance, and know him "according to Matthew," but not according to personal fellowship. Oh for a "Life of Christ" by Samuel Rutherford or George Herbert, or by some other sweet spirit to whom the everblessed One is as a familiar friend.

It is fortunate for Jesus that he commends himself to the "best thought" and ripest culture of the period; for, if he had not done so, these wise gentlemen would have exposed him as being behind the times. Of course they have every now and then to rectify certain of his dogmas, especially such as justification by faith, or atonement, or the doctrine of election—these are old-fashioned things, which belong to an older and less enlightened period, and therefore they adapt them by tearing out their real meaning. The doctrines of grace, according to the infallible critics of the period, are out of date—nobody believes them now, and so they settle off old-fashioned believers as non-existent. Christ is rectified and squared, and his garment without seam is taken off, and he is dressed out in proper style, as by a West-End clothier; then he is introduced to us as a remarkable teacher, and we are advised to accept him as far as he goes.

For the present the wise ones tolerate Jesus; but there is no telling what is to come: the progress of this age is so astonishing that it is just possible we shall before long leave Christ and Christianity behind. Now, what will come of this foolish wisdom? Nothing but delusions, mischief, infidelity, anarchy, and all manner of imaginable and unimaginable ills. The fact is, if you do not acknowledge Christ to be all, you have virtually left him out, and are without him. We must preach the Gospel, because Christ has revealed it. "Thus saith the Lord," is to be our logic. We must preach the Gospel as ambassadors delivering their message; that is to say, in the King's name, by an authority not their own. We preach our doctrines, not because we consider that they are convenient and profitable, but because Christ has commanded us to proclaim them. We believe the doctrines of grace, because they are true and are the voice of God. Age or no age has nothing to do with us. The world hates Christ and must hate him: if it would boldly denounce Christ it would be to us a more hopeful sign than its deceitful Judas kiss. We keep simply to this, the Lord hath said it, and we care not who approves or disapproves. Jesus is God and Head of the Church, and we must do what he bids us, and say what he tells us: if we fail in this, nothing of good will come of it. If the church gets back to her loyalty, she shall see what her Lord will do; but without Christ as absolute Lord, infallible Teacher, and honoured King, all must be failure even to the end.

Go a little further: you may have sound doctrine, and yet do nothing unless you have Christ *in your spirit*. I have known all the doctrines of grace to be unmistakably preached, and yet there have been no conversions; for this reason, that they were not expected and scarcely desired. In former years many orthodox preachers thought it to be their sole duty to comfort and confirm the godly few who by dint of great perseverance found out the holes and corners in which they prophesied. These brethren spoke of sinners as of people whom God might possibly gather in if he thought fit to do so; but they did not care much whether he did so or not. As to weeping over sinners as Christ wept over Jerusalem; as to venturing to invite them to Christ as the Lord did when he stretched out his hands all the day long; as to lamenting with Jeremiah over a perishing people, they had no sympathy which such emotions and feared that they savoured of Arminianism. Both preacher and congregation were cased in a hard shell, and lived as if their own salvation was the sole design of their existence. If anybody did grow zealous and seek conversions, straightway they said he was indiscreet, or conceited. When a church falls into this condition it is, as to its spirit, "without Christ." What comes of it? Some of you know by your own observation what does come of it. The comfortable corporation exists and grows for a little while, but it comes to nothing in the long run; and so it must: there can be no fruit-bearing where there is not the spirit of Christ as well as the doctrine of Christ. Except the spirit of the Lord rests upon you, causing you to agonize for the salvation of men even as Jesus did, ye can do nothing.

But above all things we must have Christ with us in the power of *his actual presence*. Do we always think of this—"Without me ye can do nothing"? We are going out this afternoon to teach the young; shall we be quite sure to take Christ with us? or on the road shall we suddenly stop and say, "I am without my Master, and I must not dare to go another step"? The abiding consciousness of the love of Christ in our souls is the essential element of our strength. We can no more convert a sinner without Christ than we could light up new stars in the sky. Power to change the human will, power to enlighten the intellect as to the things of God, and to influence the mind as to repentance and faith, must come entirely from the Most High. Do we feel that? or do we put our thoughts together for an address, and say, "Now, that is a strong point, and that will produce effect"; and do we rest there? If so, we can do nothing at all. The power lies with the Master, not with the servant; the might is in the hand, not in the weapon. We must have Christ in these pews and in these aisles, and in this pulpit, and Christ down in our Sunday School, and Christ at the street corner when we stand up there to talk of him, and we must feel that he is with us even at the end of the world, or we shall do nothing.

Now, fourthly, I hear A VOICE OF WISDOM, a still small voice which speaks out of the text, and says to us who are in Christ, *let us acknowledge this*. Down on your knees, bow your mouths in the dust and say, "Lord, it is true: without thee we can do nothing, nothing whatever that is good and acceptable in the sight of God. We have not ability of ourselves to think anything of ourselves, but our ability is of God." Now, do not speak thus, as if you paid a compliment which orthodoxy requires you to make; but from the deeps of your soul, smitten with an absolute self-despair, own the truth unto God. "To will is present with me, but how to perform that which I would I find not." Lord, I am a good-for-nothing do-nothing, a fruitless, barren, dry, rotten branch without thee, and this I feel in my inmost soul. Be not far from me, but quicken me by thy presence.

Next, *let us pray*. If without Christ we can do nothing, let us cry to him that we may never be without him. Let us with strong crying and tears entreat his abiding presence. He comes to those who seek him: let us never cease seeking. In conscious fellowship with him, let us plead that the fellowship should be unbroken evermore. Let us pray that we may be so knit and joined to Jesus that we may be one spirit with him, never to be separated from him again. Master and Lord, let the life floods of thy grace never cease to flow into us, for we know that we must be thus supplied or we can produce nothing. Let us have much more prayer than has been usual among us. Prayer is appointed to convey the blessings God ordains to give; let us constantly use the appointed means, and may the result be ever increasing from day to day.

Next, *let us personally cleave to Jesus*. Let us not attempt a life of separation; for that were to seek the living among the dead. Do not let us depart from him for a single minute. Would you like to be caught at any one second of your life in a condition in which you could do nothing? I must confess I should not like to be in that state—incapable of defence against my enemies, or of service for my Lord. If an awakened one should come before you under distress of mind, and you should feel quite incapable of doing any good to him, what a sad perplexity. Or if you did not *feel* incapable, and yet should really be so, and what if you should therefore talk on in a religious way, but know no power in it; would it not be a sad thing? May you never be in such a state that you would be a do-nothing, with opportunities afforded and yet without strength to utilize them! If you are divided from Christ you are divided from the possibility of doing good; cling, therefore, to the Saviour with your whole might, and let nothing take you off from him; no, not for an hour.

*Heartily submit yourselves*, also to the Lord's headship and leadership, and ask to do everything in his style and way. He will not be with you unless you accept him as your Master. There must be no quarrel about supremacy, but you must yield yourself up absolutely to him, to be, to do, or to suffer, according to his will. When it is wholly so he will be with you, and you shall do everything that is required of you. Wonderful things will the Lord perform through you when once he is your all in all. Will we not have it so?

Once more; *joyfully believe in him.* Though without him you can do nothing, yet with him all things are possible. Omnipotence is in that man who has Christ in him. Weakness itself you may be, but you shall learn to glory in that weakness because the power of Christ doth rest upon you if your union and communion with Christ are continually kept up. Oh for a grand confidence in Christ! We have not believed in him yet up to the measure of the hem of his garment; for even that faith made the sick woman whole. Oh to believe up to the measure of his infinite Deity! Oh for the splendour of the faith which measures itself by the Christ in whom it trusts! May God bring us there, then shall we bring forth much fruit to the glory of his name.

And now, lastly, while I was listening to my text as a child puts a shell to its ear and listens till it hears the deep sea rolling in its windings, I heard within my text A SONG OF CONTENT. "Without me ye can do nothing." My heart said, "Lord, what is there that I want to do without thee? There is no pain in this thought to me. If I can do without thee I am sorry to possess so dangerous a power. I am happy to be deprived of all strength except that which comes from thee. It charms, it exhilarates, and delights my soul to think that thou art my all. Thou hast made me penniless as to all wealth of my own, that I might dip my hand into thy treasury; thou hast taken all power away from every sinew and muscle of mine, that I may rest on thy bosom." "Without me ye can do nothing." Be it so. Are you not all agreed? Do you wish to have it altered, any of you that love his dear name? I am sure you do not; for suppose, dear friends, we could do something without Christ, then he would not have the glory of it. Who wishes that? There would be little crowns for our poor little heads, for we should have done something without him; but now there is one great crown for that dear head which once was girt with thorns; for all his saints put together cannot do anything without him. The goodly fellowship of the apostles, the noble army of martyrs, and the triumphant host of the redeemed by blood, all put together, can do nothing without Jesus. Let him be crowned with majesty who worketh in us both to will and to do of his own good pleasure.

For our own sakes, for our Lord's sake, we are glad that it is so. All things are more ours by being his; and if our fruit is his rather than our own, it is none the less but all the more ours. Is not this rare music for a holy ear?

I feel so glad that without Christ we can do nothing because I fear that if the Church could do something without Christ she would try to live without him. If she could teach the School and bring the children to salvation without Christ, I am afraid Christ would never go into a Sunday School again. If we could preach successfully without Jesus, I suspect that the Lord Jesus Christ would seldom stand on high among the people again. If our Christian literature could bless men without Christ, I am afraid we should set the printing-press going, and never think about the crucified One in the matter. Yes, it is a blessed thing for the whole Church that she must have Christ everywhere.

"Without me ye can do nothing." As I listened to the song within these words I began to laugh: I wonder if you will laugh too? I laughed, because I recollected a story of a New England service when the pastor one afternoon was preaching in his own solemn way, and the good people were listening or sleeping, as their minds inclined. It was a substantial edifice wherein they assembled, fit to outlive an earthquake. All went on peacefully in the meeting-house that afternoon till suddenly a lunatic started up, denounced the minister, and declared that he would at once pull down the meeting-house about their ears. Taking hold of one of the pillars of the gallery, this newly-announced Samson repeated his threatening. Everybody rose; the women were ready to faint; the men began to rush to the door, and there was danger that the people would be trodden on as they rushed down the aisles. There was about to be a great tumult; no one could see the end of it; when suddenly one cool brother sitting near the pulpit produced a calm by a single sentence. "Let him try!" was the stern sarcasm which hushed the tempest. Even so today the enemy is about to disprove the Gospel and crush out the doctrines of grace. Are you distressed, alarmed, astounded? So far from that, my reply to the adversary's boast that he will pull down the pillars of our Zion is this only, LET HIM TRY!

## 9

## A MESSAGE FOR THE TIME PRESENT

"In that day it shall be said to Jerusalem, Fear thou not: and to Zion, Let not thine hands be slack. The Lord thy God in the midst of thee is mighty; he will save, he will rejoice over thee with joy; he will rest in his love, he will joy over thee with singing. I will gather them that are sorrowful for the solemn assembly, who are of thee, to whom the reproach of it was a burden."—Zeph. 3: 16–18.

HOLY Scripture is wonderfully full and abiding in its inner sense. It is a springing well, whereat you may draw, and draw again; for as you draw, it springs up for ever new and fresh. It is a well of water springing up everlastingly. The fulfilment of a divine promise is not the exhaustion of it. When a man gives you a promise, and he keeps it, there is an end of the promise; but it is not so with God. When he keeps his word to the full, he has but begun; he is prepared to keep it, and keep it, and keep it for ever and ever.

What would you say of a man who had wheat upon his barn floor, and threshed it until he had beaten out the last golden grain; but the next day he went and threshed again, and brought back as much as the day before; and on the day after, again taking his flail, he went to the same threshing, and again brought back his measure as full as at the first, and so on for all the days of the year? Would it not seem to you as a fairy tale? It would certainly be a surprising miracle.

But what should we say if, throughout a long life, this miracle could be prolonged? Yet we have continued to thresh the promises ever since faith was given us, and we have carried away our full portion every day. What shall we say of the glorious fact that the saints in all generations, from the first day until now, have done the same; and of that equal truth, that as long as there is a needy soul upon earth, there will be upon the threshing floor of the promises the same abundance of the finest wheat as when the first man filled his measure and returned rejoicing? I will not dwell upon the specific application of the text before us: I do not doubt that it was specially fulfilled as it was intended; and if there still remains some special piece of history to which this passage alludes, it will again be fulfilled in due time; but this I know, that those who have lived between whiles have found this promise true to them. Children of God have used these promises under all sorts of circumstances, and have derived the utmost comfort from them. Let our prayer then be that we may enjoy this marvellous portion of the sacred word, and take intense delight in it. As God rests in his love, so may we rest in it now; and as he joys over us with singing, so may we break forth into joyous psalms to the God of our salvation.

I am going to begin with the last verse of the text, and work my way upwards. The first head is, *a trying day for God's people.* They are sorrowful because a cloud is upon their solemn assembly, and the reproach thereof is a burden. Secondly, we will note *a glorious ground of consolation.* We read in the seventeenth verse, "The Lord thy God in the midst of thee is mighty; he will save, he will rejoice over thee with joy; he will rest in his love, he will joy with thee over singing." And, thirdly, here is *a brave conduct suggested thereby*: "In that day it shall be said to Jerusalem, Fear thou not: and to Zion, Let not thine hands be slack."

Beginning at the eighteenth verse, we notice A TRYING DAY FOR GOD'S PEOPLE. *The solemn assembly had fallen under reproach.* The solemn assemblies of Israel were her glory: her great days of festival and sacrifice were the gladness of the land. To the faithful their holy days were their holidays. But a reproach had fallen upon the solemn assembly, and I believe it is so now at this present moment. It is a sad affliction when in our solemn assemblies *the brilliance of the Gospel light is dimmed by error.* The clearness of the testimony is spoiled when doubtful voices are scattered among the people, and those who ought to preach the truth, the whole truth, and nothing but the truth, are telling out for doctrines the imaginations of men, and the inventions of the age. Instead of revelation, we have philosophy, falsely so-called; instead of divine infallibility, we have surmises and larger hopes. The Gospel of Jesus Christ, which is the same yesterday, today, and for ever, is taught as the production of progress, a growth, a thing to be amended and corrected year by year. It is an ill day, both for the Church and the world, when the trumpet does not give a certain sound; for who shall prepare himself for the battle?

If added to this we should see *creeping over the solemn assembly of the Church a lifelessness, an indifference, and a lack of spiritual power*, it is painful to a high degree. When the vitality of religion is despised, and gatherings for prayer are neglected, what are we coming to? The present period of Church history is well portrayed by the Church of Laodicea, which was neither cold nor hot, and therefore to be spewed out of Christ's mouth. That Church gloried that she was rich and increased in goods, and had need of nothing, while all the while her Lord was outside, knocking at the door, a door closed against him. That passage is constantly applied to the unconverted, with whom it has nothing to do: it had to do with a lukewarm Church, with a Church that thought itself to be in an eminently prosperous condition, while her living Lord, in the doctrine of his atoning sacrifice, was denied an entrance. Oh, if he had found admission—and he was eager to find it—she would soon have flung away her imaginary wealth, and he would have given her gold tried in the furnace, and white raiment with which she might be clothed. Alas! she is content without her Lord, for she has education, oratory, science, and a thousand other baubles. Zion's solemn assembly is under a cloud, indeed, when the teaching of Jesus and his apostles is of small account with her.

If in addition to this, *worldly conformity spreads in the church*, so that the vain amusements of the world are shared in by the saints, then is there reason enough for lamentation, even as Jeremiah cried: "How is the gold become dim!" Her Nazarites, who were purer than snow and whiter than milk, have become blacker than a coal. "All our enemies have opened their mouths against us." If no longer there is a clear distinction between the Church and the world, but professed followers of Jesus have joined hands with unbelievers, then may we mourn indeed! Woe worth the day! An ill time has happened to the Church and to the world also. We may expect great judgments, for the Lord will surely be avenged on such a people as this.

It appears from the text that *there were some to whom the*

*reproach was a burden.* They could not make sport of sin. True, there were many who said that the evil did not exist at all, and others who declared that it was not present in any great degree. Yes, and more hardened spirits declared that what was considered to be a reproach was really a thing to be boasted of, the very glory of the century. Thus they huffed the matter, and made the mourning of the conscientious to be a theme for jest. But there was a remnant to whom the reproach of it was a burden; these could not bear to see such a calamity. To these the Lord God will have respect, as he said by the prophet: "Go through the midst of the city, through the midst of Jerusalem, and set a mark upon the foreheads of the men that sigh and that cry for all the abominations that be done in the midst thereof." The many drank wine in bowls and anointed themselves with their chief ointments, but they were not grieved for the affliction of Joseph (Amos 6: 6); but these were pressed in spirit and bore the cross, counting the reproach of Christ greater riches than all the treasures of Egypt. God's people cannot bear that Christ's atoning sacrifice should be dishonoured; they cannot endure that his truth should be trodden as mire in the streets. To true believers prosperity means the Holy Ghost blessing the word to the conversion of sinners and the building up of saints; and if they do not see this, they hang their harps upon the willows. True lovers of Jesus fast when the Bridegroom is not with his Church: their glory is in his glory, and in nothing else. The wife of Phinehas, the son of Eli, cried out in her dying agony, "The glory has departed," and the reason that she gave was once because of the death of her husband and his father, but twice because "the ark of God is taken." For this she named her new-born child Ichabod—"The glory is departed from Israel, for the ark of God is taken." The bitterest pain of this godly woman was for the Church, and for the honour of our God. So it is with God's true people: they lay it much to heart that the truth is rejected.

This burdened spirit is a token of true love to God: those who love the Lord Jesus are wounded in his woundings, and vexed with the vexings of his Spirit. When Christ is dishonoured his disciples are dishonoured. Those who have a tender heart towards the Church can say with Paul: "Who is offended, and

I burn not?" The sins of the Church of God are the sorrows of all living members of it. This also marks a healthy sensibility, a vital spirituality. Those who are unspiritual care nothing for truth or grace: they look to finances, and numbers, and respectability. But men whose spirits are of God would sooner see the faithful persecuted than see them desert the truth, sooner see churches in the depths of poverty full of holy zeal than rich churches dead in worldliness. Spiritual men care for the Church even when she is in an evil case, and cast down by her adversaries: "thy servants take pleasure in her stones, and favour the dust thereof." The house of the Lord is to many of us our own house, his family is our family. Unless the Lord Jesus be extolled, and his Gospel conquer, we feel that our own personal interests are blighted, and we ourselves are in disgrace. It is no small thing to us: it is our life.

Thus have I dwelt upon the fact that it is an ill day for God's people when the solemn assembly is defiled: the reproach thereof is a burden to those who are truly citizens of the New Jerusalem, and because of this *they are seen to be sorrowful.* The Lord here says, "I will gather them that are sorrowful for the solemn assembly." They may well be sorrowful when such a burden is laid on their hearts. Moreover, they see in a hundred ways the ill effect of the evil which they deplore. Many are lame and halting; this is hinted at in the promise of the nineteenth verse: "I will save her that halteth." Pilgrims on the road to Zion were made to limp on the road because the prophets were "light and treacherous persons." When the pure Gospel is not preached, God's people are robbed of the strength which they need in their life-journey. If you take away the bread, the children hunger. If you give the flock poisonous pastures, or fields which are barren as the desert, they pine and they become lame in their daily following of the shepherd. The doctrinal soon affects the practical. I know many of the people of God living in different parts of this country to whom the Sabbath is very little of a day of rest, for they hear no truth in which rest is to be found, but they are worried and wearied with novelties which neither glorify God nor benefit the souls of men. In many a place the sheep look up and are not fed.

This causes much disquietude and breeds doubts and

questionings, and thus strength is turned to weakness, and the work of faith, the labour of love, and the patience of hope are all kept in a halting state. This is a grievous evil, and it is all around us. Then, alas! many are "driven out," of whom the nineteenth verse says, "I will gather her that was driven out." By false doctrine many are made to wander from the fold. Hopeful ones are made to stray from the path of life, and sinners are left in their natural distance from God. The truth which would convince men of sin is not preached, while other truths which would lead seekers into peace are beclouded, and souls are left in needless sorrow. When the doctrines of grace and the glorious atoning sacrifice are not set clearly before men's minds, so that they may feel their power, all sorts of evils follow. It is terrible to me that this dreadful blight should come upon our churches; for the hesitating are driven to destruction, the weak are staggered, and even the strong are perplexed. The false teachers of these days would, if it were possible, deceive the very elect. This makes our hearts very sorrowful. How can we help it?

Yet, all the time that the people of God are in this evil case, *they are not without hope;* for close upon all this comes the promise of the Lord to restore his wandering ones. We have the sense twice over: "I will get them praise and fame in every land where they have been put to shame." "I will make you a name and a praise among all people of the earth, when I turn back your captivity before your eyes, saith the Lord." The adversaries cannot silence the eternal testimony. They hanged our Lord himself upon a tree; they took down his body and buried it in a tomb in the rock; and they set their seal upon the stone which they rolled at the mouth of the sepulchre. Surely now there was an end of the Christ and his cause. Boast not, ye priests and Pharisees! Vain the watch, the stone, the seal! When the appointed time had come, the living Christ came forth. He could not be holden by the cords of death. How idle their dreams! "He that sitteth in the heavens shall laugh: the Lord doth have them in derision." Beloved, the reproach will yet be rolled away from the solemn assembly: the truth of God will yet again be proclaimed as with trumpet tongue, the Spirit of God will revive his Church, and converts as many as the sheaves of the harvest shall yet be gathered in.

How will the faithful rejoice! Those who were burdened and sorrowful shall then put on their garments of joy and beauty. Then shall the ransomed of the Lord return with songs and everlasting joy upon their heads. The conflict is not doubtful. The end of the battle is sure and certain. Methinks I even now hear the shout, "The Lord God omnipotent reigneth."

Secondly, let us think of something which shines like a star amid the darkness. The second verse of the text presents a GLORIOUS GROUND OF CONSOLATION. Here is a rich text indeed. This passage is like a great sea, while I am as a little child making pools in the sand which skirts its boundless flood. A series of discourses might well be founded on this seventeenth verse.

*Our great consolation in the worst times lies in our God.* The very name of our covenant God—"the Lord thy God"—is full of good cheer. That word, "the Lord," is really JEHOVAH, the self-existent One, the unchangeable One, the ever-living God, who cannot change or be moved from his everlasting purpose. Children of God, whatever you have not got, you have a God in whom you may greatly glory. Having God you have more than all things, for all things come of him; and if all things were blotted out, he could restore all things simply by his will. He speaketh, and it is done; he commandeth, and it stands fast. Blessed is the man that hath the God of Jacob for his trust, and whose hope Jehovah is. In the Lord Jehovah we have righteousness and strength; let us trust in him for ever. Let the times roll on, they cannot affect our God. Let troubles rush upon us like a tempest, but they shall not come nigh unto us now that he is our defence.

Jehovah, the God of his Church, is also the God of each individual member of it, and each one may therefore rejoice in him. Jehovah is as much your God, as if no other person in the universe could use that covenant expression. O believer, the Lord God is altogether and wholly your God! All his wisdom, all his foresight, all his power, all his immutability—all himself is yours. As for the Church of God, when she is in her lowest estate she is still established and endowed in the best possible sense—established by the divine decree, and endowed by the possession of God all-sufficient. The gates of hell shall not prevail against her. Let us exult in our possession.

Poor as we are, we are infinitely rich in having God; weak as we are, there is no limit to our strength, since the Almighty Jehovah is ours. "If God be for us, who can be against us? If God be ours, what more can we need? Lift up thy heart, thou sorrowful one, and be of good cheer. If God be thy God, thou hast all thou canst desire: wrapped up within his glorious name, we find all things for time and eternity, for earth and heaven. Therefore in the name of Jehovah we will set up our banners, and march onward to the battle. He is our God by his own purpose, covenant, and oath; and this day he is our God by our own choice of him, by our union with Christ Jesus, by our experience of his goodness, and by that spirit of adoption whereby we cry "Abba, Father."

To strengthen this consolation, we notice next, that *this God is in the midst of us.* He is not a long way off, to be sought with difficulty, if haply we may find him. Our God is "Jehovah in the midst of thee." Since that bright night in which a Babe was born at Bethlehem, and unto us a Son was given, we know God as "Emmanuel, God with us." God is in our nature, and therefore very near unto us. "The Word was made flesh, and dwelt among us." Though his bodily presence is gone, yet we have his spiritual presence with us evermore; for he saith, "Lo, I am with you alway." He walketh among the golden candlesticks. We have also the immediate presence of God, the Holy Spirit. He is in the midst of the Church to enlighten, convince, quicken, endow, comfort, and clothe with spiritual power. The Lord still works in the minds of men for the accomplishment of his purposes of grace. Let us think of this when we are going forth to Christian service; "The Lord of hosts is with us." When you call your class together in the Sabbath School, say to your Lord, "If thy presence go not with me, carry me not up hence." If we have God with us, we can bear to be deserted by men. What a word that is, "Where two or three are gathered together in my name, there am I in the midst of them!" Shall not the army shout when the King himself is in their ranks! Let God arise, let his enemies be scattered! When he is with us they that hate him must flee before him. Be it our concern so to love that we may never grieve away the Spirit of God. Beloved, there is such abundant consolation in the fact of the presence of God with us, that if we could only feel the power of it at this moment, we should enter into rest, and our heaven would begin below.

Let us go a step further, and note that our consolation is largely to be found in the fact that *this God in the midst of us is full of power to save.* "The Lord thy God in the midst of thee is mighty; he will save." That is to say, "Jehovah, thy God, is mighty to save." His arm is not shortened, he is still "a just God and a Saviour." Nor is he merely able to save, but he will display that ability; "he will save." Let us pray, then, that he *will* save; that he will save his own Church from lukewarmness and from deadly error; that He will save her from her worldliness and formalism; from unconverted ministers and ungodly members. Let us lift up our eyes and behold the power which is ready to save; and let us go on to pray that the Lord may save the unconverted by thousands and millions.

Oh, that we might see a great revival of religion. This is what we want before all things. This would smite the enemy upon the cheek-bone, and break the teeth of the adversary. If tens of thousands of souls were immediately saved by the sovereign grace of God, what a rebuke it would be to those who deny the faith! Oh, for times such as our fathers saw when first Whitefield and his helpers began to preach the life-giving word! When one sweet voice was heard clear and loud, all the birds of paradise began to sing in concert with him, and the morning of a glorious day was heralded. If we are importunate in prayer it must happen: "God shall bless us, and all the ends of the earth shall fear him." Let us not seek power of rhetoric, much less of wealth; but let us look for the power which saves.

This is the one thing I crave. Oh, that God would save souls! I say to myself, after being badgered and worried through the week by the men of modern thought: "I will go my way and preach Christ's Gospel, and win souls." One lifting up of Jesus Christ crucified is more to me than all the cavillings of the men who are wise above what is written. Converts are our unanswerable arguments. "Happy is the man," saith the Psalm, "that hath his quiver full of them: they shall speak with the enemies in the gate." Blessed is the man who has many spiritual children born to God under his ministry; for his converts are his defence. Beholding the man who was healed standing with

Peter and John, they could say nothing against them. If souls are saved by the Gospel, the Gospel is proved in the surest manner. Let us care more about conversions than about organizations. If souls are brought into union with Christ, we may let other unions go.

We go yet further, and we come to great deeps: behold *God's joy in his people.* "He will rejoice over thee with joy." Think of this! Jehovah, the living God, is described as brooding over his Church with pleasure. He looks upon souls redeemed by the blood of his dear Son, quickened by his Holy Spirit, and his heart is glad. Even the infinite heart of God is filled with an extraordinary joy at the sight of his chosen. His delight is in his Church, his Hephzibah. I can understand a minister rejoicing over a soul that he has brought to Christ; I can also understand believers rejoicing to see others saved from sin and hell; but what shall I say of the infinitely-happy and eternally-blessed God finding, as it were, a new joy in souls redeemed? This is another of those great wonders which cluster around the work of divine grace! "He will rejoice over thee with joy." Oh, you are trembling for the ark of the Lord; the Lord is not trembling, but rejoicing. Faulty as the Church is, the Lord rejoices in her. While we mourn, as well we may, yet we do not sorrow as those that are without hope; for God does not sorrow, his heart is glad, and he is said to rejoice with joy—a highly emphatic expression. The Lord taketh pleasure in them that fear him, imperfect though they be. He sees them as they are to be, and so he rejoices over them, even when they cannot rejoice in themselves. When your face is blurred with tears, your eyes red with weeping, and your heart heavy with sorrow for sin, the great Father is rejoicing over you. The prodigal son wept in his Father's bosom, but the Father rejoiced over his son. We are questioning, doubting, sorrowing, trembling; and all the while he who sees the end from the beginning knows what will come out of the present disquietude, and therefore rejoices. Let us rise in faith to share the joy of God. Let no man's heart fail him because of the taunts of the enemy. Rather let the chosen of God rouse themselves to courage, and participate in that joy of God which never ceaseth, even though the solemn assembly has become a reproach. Shall we not rejoice in him when he, in his boundless condescension, deigns to rejoice in us? Whoever despairs for the cause, he does not; wherefore let us be of good courage.

It is added, "*He will rest in his love.*" I do not know any Scripture which is more full of wonderful meaning than this. "He will rest in his love," as if our God had in his people found satisfaction. He comes to an anchorage: he has reached his desire. Jesus sees of the travail of his soul when his people are won to him; he has been baptized with his baptism for his Church, and he is no longer straitened, for his desire is fulfilled. The Lord is content with his eternal choice, content with his loving purposes, satisfied with the love which went forth from everlasting. He is well pleased in Jesus—well pleased with all the glorious purposes which are connected with his dear Son, and with those who are in him. He has a calm content in the people of his choice, as he sees them in Christ. This is a good ground for our having a deep satisfaction of heart also. We are not what we would be; but then we are not what we shall be. We advance slowly; but then we advance surely. The end is secured by omnipotent grace. It is right that we should be discontented with ourselves, yet this holy restlessness should not rob us of our perfect peace in Christ Jesus. If the Lord hath rest in us, shall we not have rest in him? If he rests in his love, cannot we rest in it? My heart is comforted as I plainly see in these words love unchanging, love abiding, love eternal: "he will rest in his love." Jehovah changes not. Our Lord died for his Church, and so long as he lives he will remember his own love, and what it cost him: "Who shall separate us from the love of God which is in Christ Jesus our Lord?" "He will rest in his love."

The love of God to us is undisturbed: "The peace of God, which passeth all understanding," dwells with his love: he is not disquieted about it, but peacefully loves, and is never moved. The calm of God is wonderful to contemplate: his infallible knowledge and infinite power put him beyond fear or question. He sees no cause of alarm as to his redeemed, nor as to the cause of truth and the reign of righteousness. As to his true Church, he knows that she is right, or that he will make her right. She is being transformed into the image of Jesus, and he rests in the full assurance that the image will ere long be complete. He can carry out his own purposes in his own way and time. He can see the harvest as well as the sowing; therefore he doth "rest in his love." You have seen a mother wash her child, and as she washes its face the child perhaps is crying, for it does not for the present enjoy the cleansing operation. Does the mother share the child's grief? Does she also cry? Oh, no! she rejoices over her babe, and rests in her love, knowing that the light affliction of the little one will work its real good. Often our griefs are no deeper than the cry of a child because of the soap in its eyes. While the Church is being washed with tribulations and persecutions, God is resting in his love. You and I are wearying, but God is resting.

"He will rest in his love." The Hebrew of this line is, "He shall be silent in his love." His happiness in his love is so great, that he does not express it, but keeps a happy silence. His is a joy too deep for words. No language can express the joy of God in his love; and therefore he uses no words. Silence in this case is infinitely expressive. One of the old commentators says, "He is deaf and dumb in his love," as if he heard no voice of accusation against his chosen, and would not speak a word of upbraiding to her. Remember the silence of Jesus, and expound this text thereby.

Sometimes also the Lord does not speak to his people: we cannot get a cheering word from him; and then we sigh for a promise, and long for a visit of his love; but if he be thus silent, let us know that he is only silent in his love. It is not the silence of wrath, but of love. His love is not changed, even though he does not comfort us.

*His thoughts are high, his love is wise,*
*His wounds a cure intend;*
*And though he does not always smile,*
*He loves unto the end.*

When he does not answer our prayers with his hand, he yet hears them with his heart. Denials are only another form of the same love which grants our petitions. He loves us, and sometimes shows that love better by not giving us what we ask than he could do if he spoke the sweetest promise which the ear has ever heard. I prize this sentence: "He will rest in his love."

My God, thou art perfectly content with thy Church after all, because thou knowest what she is to be. Thou seest how fair she will be when she comes forth from the washing, having put on her beautiful garments. Lo, the sun goes down, and we mortals dread the endless darkness; but thou, great God, seest the morning, and thou knowest that in the hours of darkness dews will fall which shall refresh thy garden. Ours is the measure of an hour, and thine the judgment of eternity, therefore we will correct our short-sighted judgment by thine infallible knowledge, and rest with thee.

The last word is, however, the most wonderful of all: "*He will joy over thee with singing.*" Think of the great Jehovah singing! Can you imagine it? Is it possible to conceive of the Deity breaking into a song: Father, Son and Holy Ghost together singing over the redeemed? God is so happy in the love which he bears to his people that he breaks the eternal silence, and sun and moon and stars with astonishment hear God chanting a hymn of joy. Among Orientals a certain song is sung by the bridegroom when he receives his bride: it is intended to declare his joy in her, and in the fact that his marriage has come. Here, by the pen of inspiration, the God of love is pictured as married to his Church, and so rejoicing in her that he rejoices over her with singing.

If God sings, shall not we sing? He did not sing when he made the world. No; he looked upon it, and simply said that it was good. The angels sang, the sons of God shouted for joy: creation was very wonderful to them, but it was not much to God, who could have made thousands of worlds by his mere will. Creation could not make him sing; and I do not even know that Providence ever brought a note of joy from him, for he could arrange a thousand kingdoms of providence with ease. But when it came to redemption, that cost him dear. Here he spent eternal thought and drew up a covenant with infinite wisdom. Here he gave his Only-begotten Son and put him to grief to ransom his beloved ones. When all was done, and the Lord saw what became of it in the salvation of his redeemed, then he rejoiced after a divine manner. What must the joy be which recompenses Gethsemane and Calvary! The Lord God receives an accession to the infinity of his joy in the thought of his redeemed people. "He shall rejoice over thee with singing." I tremble while I speak of such themes, lest I should say a word that should dishonour the matchless mystery; but still we are glad to note what is written, and we are bound to take comfort from it. Let us have sympathy with the joy of the Lord, for this will be our strength.

I close with a brief word upon THE BRAVE CONDUCT SUGGESTED THEREBY. Let us not sorrow under the burdens which we bear, but rejoice in God, the great Burden-bearer, upon whom this day we roll our load. Here it is—"In that day it shall be said to Jerusalem, Fear thou not; and to Zion, Let not thine hands be slack."

There are three things for God's people to do. The first is, to *be happy*. Read verse fourteen—"Sing, O daughter of Zion; shout, O Israel; be glad and rejoice with all thy heart, O daughter of Jerusalem." Any man can sing when his cup is full of delights; the believer alone has songs when waters of a bitter cup are wrung out to him. Any sparrow can chirp in the daylight; it is only the nightingale that can sing in the dark. Children of God, whenever the enemies seem to prevail over you, whenever the serried ranks of the foe appear sure of victory, then begin to sing. Your victory will come with your song. It is a very puzzling thing to the devil to hear saints sing when he sets his foot on them. He cannot make it out: the more he oppresses them, the more they rejoice. Let us resolve to be all the merrier when the enemy dreams that we are utterly routed. The more opposition, the more we will rejoice in the Lord; the more discouragement, the more confidence. Splendid was the courage of Alexander when they told him that there were hundreds of thousands of Persians. "Yet," he said, "one butcher fears not myriads of sheep." "Ah!" said another, "when the Persians draw their bows, their arrows are so numerous that they darken the sun." "It will be fine to fight in the shade," cried the hero.

O friends, we know whom we have believed, and we are sure of triumph! Let us not think for a single second, if the odds against us are ten thousand to one, that this is a hardship; rather let us wish that they were a million to one, that the glory of the Lord might be all the greater in the conquest which is sure.

When Athanasius was told that everybody was denying the Deity of Christ, then he said, "I, Athanasius, against the world": *Athanasius contra mundum* became a proverbial expression. It is a splendid thing to be quite alone in the warfare of the Lord. Suppose we had half-a-dozen with us. Six men are not much increase to strength, and possibly they may be a cause of weakness, by needing to be looked after. If you are quite alone, so much the better: there is the more room for God. When desertions have cleaned the place out, and left you no friend, now every corner can be filled with Deity, "for great is the Holy One of Israel in the midst of thee."

The next duty is *fearlessness*: "Fear thou not." What! not a little? No, "Fear thou not." But surely I may show some measure of trembling? No, "Fear thou not." Tie that knot tight about the throat of unbelief. "Fear thou not": neither this day, nor any day of thy life. When fear comes in, drive it away; give it no space. If God rests in his love, and if God sings, what canst thou have to do with fear? Have you never known passengers on board ship, when the weather was rough, comforted by the calm behaviour of the captain? One simple-minded soul said to his friend, "I am sure there is no cause for fear, for I heard the captain whistling." Surely, if the captain is at ease, and with him is all the responsibility, the passenger may be still more at peace. If the Lord Jesus at the helm is singing, let us not be fearing. Let us have done with every timorous accent. O rest in the Lord, and wait patiently for him. "Your God will come with vengeance, even God with a recompense; he will come and save you."

Lastly, let us *be zealous*: "Let not thine hands be slack." Now is the time when every Christian should do more for God than ever. Let us plan great things for God, and let us expect great things from God. "Let not thine hands be slack." Now is the hour for redoubled prayers and labours. Since the adversaries are busy, let us be busy also. If they think they shall make a full end of us, let us resolve to make a full end of their falsehoods and delusions. I think every Christian man should answer the challenge of the adversaries of Christ by working double tides, by giving more of his substance to the cause of God, by living more for the glory of God, by being more exact in his obedience, more earnest in his efforts, and more importunate in his prayers. "Let not thine hands be slack." in any one part of holy service.

## 10

## OUR URGENT NEED OF THE HOLY SPIRIT

"Through the power of the Holy Ghost."—Rom. 15: 13.
"By the power of the Spirit of God."—Rom. 15: 19.

I DESIRE to draw your attention at this time to the great necessity which exists for the continual manifestation of the power of the Holy Spirit in the Church of God if by her means the multitudes are to be gathered to the Lord Jesus. I did not know how I could much better do so than by first showing that the Spirit of God is necessary to the Church of God for its own internal growth in grace. Hence my text in the thirteenth verse, "Now the God of hope fill you with all joy and peace in believing, that ye may abound in hope, through the power of the Holy Ghost," where it is evident that the apostle attributes the power to be filled with joy and peace in believing, and the power to abound in hope, to the Holy Ghost. But, then, I wanted also to show you that the power of the Church outside, that with which she is to be aggressive and work upon the world for the gathering out of God's elect from among men, is also this same energy of the Holy Spirit. Hence I have taken the nineteenth verse, for the apostle there says that God had through him made "the Gentiles obedient by word and deed, through mighty signs and wonders, by the power of the Spirit of God." So you see that first of all to keep the Church happy and holy within herself there must be a manifestation of the power of the Holy Spirit, and secondly, that the Church may invade the territories of the enemy and may conquer the world for Christ she must be clothed with the self-same sacred energy. We may then go further and say that the power of the Church for external work will be proportionate to the power which dwells within herself. Gauge the energy of the Holy Spirit in the hearts of believers, and you may fairly calculate their influence upon unbelievers. Only let the Church be illuminated by the Holy Spirit and she will reflect the light and become to onlookers "fair as the moon, clear as the sun, and terrible as an army with banners."

Let us by two illustrations show that the work outward must always depend upon the force inward. On a cold winter's day when the snow has fallen and lies deep upon the ground you go through a village. There is a row of cottages, and you will notice that from one of the roofs the snow has nearly disappeared, while another cottage still bears a coating of snow. You do not stay to make enquiries as to the reason for the difference, for you know very well what is the cause. There is a fire burning inside the one cottage and the warmth glows through its roof, and so the snow speedily melts: in the other there is no tenant; it is a house to let, no fire burns on its hearth and no warm smoke ascends the chimney, and therefore there lies the snow. Just as the warmth is within, so the melting will be without. I look at a number of Churches, and where I see worldliness and formalism lying thick upon them, I am absolutely certain that there is not the warmth of Christian life within; but where the hearts of believers are warm with divine love through the Spirit of God, we are sure to see evils vanish, and beneficial consequences following therefrom.

Take another illustration. If you lived in Egypt, you would notice, once in the year, the Nile rising; and you would watch its increase with anxiety, because the extent of the overflow of the Nile is very much the measure of the fertility of Egypt. Now the rising of the Nile must depend upon those far-off lakes in the centre of Africa—whether they shall be well filled with the melting of the snows or no. If there be a scanty supply in the higher reservoirs, there cannot be much overflow in the Nile in its after-course through Egypt. Let us translate the figure, and say that, if the upper lakes of fellowship with God in the Christian Church are not well filled—if the soul's spiritual strength be not sustained by private prayer and communion with God—the Nile of practical Christian service will never rise to the flood.

The one thing I want to say is this: you cannot get out of the Church what is not in it. The reservoir itself must be filled before it can pour forth a stream. We must ourselves drink of the living water till we are full, and then out of the midst of us shall flow rivers of living water; but not till then. Out of an empty basket you cannot distribute loaves and fishes, however hungry the crowd may be. Out of the fulness of the heart the mouth speaketh, when it speaks to edification at all. So that the first thing is to look well to home affairs, and pray that God would bless *us* and cause his face to shine upon *us*, that his way may be known upon earth, and his saving health among all people.

*To bless thy chosen race,*
*In mercy, Lord, incline,*
*And cause the brightness of thy face*
*On all thy saints to shine.*

*That so thy wondrous way*
*May through the world be known;*
*Whilst distant lands their tribute pay,*
*And thy salvation own.*

In trying to speak of the great necessity of the Church, namely, her being moved vigorously by the power of the Holy Spirit, I earnestly pray that we may enter upon this subject with the deepest conceivable reverence. Let us adore while we are meditating; let us feel the condescension of this blessed Person of the Godhead in deigning to dwell in his people and to work in the human heart. Let us remember that this divine person is very sensitive. He is a jealous God. We read of his being grieved and vexed, and therefore let us ask his forgiveness of the many provocations which he must have received from our hands. With lowliest awe let us bow before him, remembering that, if there be a sin which is unpardonable, it has a reference to himself—the sin against the Holy Ghost, which shall never be forgiven, neither in this world nor in that which is to come. In reference to the Holy Ghost we stand on very tender ground indeed; and if ever we should veil our faces and rejoice with trembling, it is while we speak of the Spirit, and of those mysterious works with which he blesses us. In that lowly spirit, and under the divine overshadowing follow me while I set before you seven works of the Holy Spirit which are most necessary to the Church for its own good, and equally needful to her in her office of missionary from Christ to the outside world.

To begin, then, the power of the Holy Ghost is manifested in the QUICKENING of souls to spiritual life. All the spiritual life which exists in this world is the creation of the Holy Spirit, by whom the Lord Jesus quickeneth whomsoever he will. You and I had not life enough to know our death till he visited us, we had not light enough to perceive that we were in darkness, nor sense enough to feel our misery: we were so utterly abandoned to our own folly that, though we were naked and poor, and miserable, we dreamed that we were rich, and increased in goods. We were under sentence of death as condemned criminals, and yet we talked about merit and reward; yea, we were dead, and yet we boasted that we were alive—counting our very death to be our life. The Spirit of God in infinite mercy came to us with his mysterious power, and made us live. The first token of life was a consciousness of our being in the realm of death, and an agony to escape from it; we began to perceive our insensibility, and, if I may be pardoned such an expression, we saw our blindness. Every growth of spiritual life, from the first tender shoot until now, has also been the work of the Holy Spirit. As the green blade was his production, so is the ripening corn. The increase of life, as much as life at the beginning, must still come by the operation of the Spirit of God, who raised up Christ from the dead. You will never have more life except as the Holy Ghost bestows it upon you; yea, you will not even know that you want more, nor groan after more, except as he worketh in you to desire and to agonise, according to his own good pleasure. See, then, our absolute dependence upon the Holy Spirit; for if he were gone we should relapse into spiritual death, and the Church would become a charnel-house.

The Holy Spirit is absolutely needful to make everything that we do to be alive. We are sowers, but if we take dead seed in our seed-basket there will never be a harvest. The preacher must preach living truth in a living manner if he expects to obtain a hundred-fold harvest. How much there is of Church work which is nothing better than the movement of a galvanized corpse. How much of religion is done as if it were performed by an automaton, or ground off by machinery. Now-a-days men care little about heart and soul, they only look at outward performances. Men can give mechanically, and come to the communion table mechanically: yes, and we ourselves shall do so unless the Spirit of God be with us. Most hearers know what it is to hear a live sermon which quivers all over with fulness of energy; you also know what it is to sing a hymn in a lively manner, and you know what it is to unite in a live prayer meeting; but, ah, if the Spirit of God be absent, all that the Church does will be lifeless, the rustle of leaves above a tomb.

As the Spirit of God is a quickener to make us alive and our work alive, so must he specially be with us to make those alive with whom we have to deal for Jesus. Imagine a dead preacher preaching a dead sermon to dead sinners: what can possibly come of it? Here is a beautiful essay which has been admirably elaborated, and it is coldly read to the cold-hearted sinner. It smells of the midnight oil, but it has no heavenly unction, no divine power resting upon it, nor, perhaps, is that power even looked for. What good can come of such a production? As well may you try to calm the tempest with poetry or stay the hurricane with rhetoric as to bless a soul by mere learning and eloquence. It is only as the Spirit of God shall come upon God's servant and shall make the word which he preaches to drop as a living seed into the heart that any result can follow his ministry; and it is only as the Spirit of God shall then follow that seed and keep it alive in the soul of the listener that we can expect those who profess to be converted to take root and grow to maturity of grace, and become our sheaves at the last.

We are utterly dependent here, and for my part I rejoice in this absolute dependence. If I could have a stock of power to save souls which would be all my own apart from the Spirit of God, I cannot suppose a greater temptation to pride and to living at a distance from God. It is well to be weak in self, and better still to be nothing: to be simply the pen in the hand of the Spirit of God, unable to write a single letter upon the tablets of the human heart except as the hand of the Holy Spirit shall use us for that purpose. That is really our position, and we ought practically to take it up; and doing so we shall continually cry to the Spirit of God to quicken us in all things, and quicken all that we do, and quicken the word as it drops into the sinner's ear. I am quite certain that a Church which is devoid of life cannot be the means of life-giving to the dead sinners around it. No. Everything acts after its kind, and we must have a living Church for living work. Oh that God would quicken every member of this Church! "What," say you, "do you think some of us are not alive unto God?" There are some of you concerning whom I am certain, as far as one can judge of another, that you have life, for we can see it in all that you do; but there are some others of you concerning whose spiritual life one has to exercise a good deal of faith and a great deal more charity, for we do not perceive in you much activity in God's cause, nor care for the souls of others, nor zeal for the divine glory. If we do not see any fruits, what can we do but earnestly pray that you may not turn out to be barren trees?

Next it is one of the peculiar offices of the Holy Spirit to ENLIGHTEN his people. He has done so by giving us his Word, which he has inspired; but the Book, inspired though it be, is never spiritually understood by any man apart from the personal teaching of its great Author. You may read it as much as you will, and never discover the inner and vital sense unless your soul shall be led into it by the Holy Ghost himself. The Spirit of God must come and make the letter of truth alive to you, transfer it to your heart, set it on fire and make it burn within you, or else its divine force and majesty will be hid from your eyes. No man knows the things of God save he to whom the Spirit of God has revealed them. We may use language as plain as a pikestaff, but the man who has no spiritual understanding is a blind man, and the clearest light will not enable him to see. Ye must be taught of the Lord, or you will die in ignorance. Now, suppose that in a Church there should be many who have never been thus instructed, can you not see that evil must and will come of it? Error is sure to arise where truth is not experimentally known. Half of the heresy in the Church of God is not wilful error, but error which springs of not knowing the truth, not searching the Scriptures with a teachable heart, not submitting the mind to the light of the Holy Ghost. We should, as a rule, treat heresy rather as ignorance to be enlightened than as crime to be condemned; save, alas, that sometimes it becomes wilful perversity, when the mind is greedy after novelty, or puffed up with self-confidence: then other treatment may become painfully necessary. Beloved, if the Spirit of God will but enlighten the

Church thoroughly there will be an end of divisions. Schisms are generally occasioned by ignorance, and the proud spirit which will not brook correction. On the other hand, real, lasting, practical unity will exist in proportion to the unity of men's minds in the truth of God. Hence the necessity for the Spirit of God to conduct us into the whole truth. If you think you know a doctrine, ask the Lord to make sure that you know it, for much that we think we know turns out to be unknown when times of trial put us to the test. Nothing do we really know unless it be burnt into our souls as with a hot iron by an experience which only the Spirit of God can give.

I think you will now see that, the Spirit of God being thus necessary, for our instruction, we pre-eminently find in this gracious operation our strength for the instruction of others; for how shall those teach who have never been taught? How shall men declare a message which they have never learned? "Son of man, eat this roll"; for until thou hast eaten it thyself thy lips can never tell it out to others. "The husbandman that laboureth must first be a partaker of the fruits." It is the law of Christ's vineyard that none shall work therein till first of all they know the flavour of the fruits which grow in the sacred enclosure. Thou must know Christ, and grace, and love, and truth thyself before thou canst even be an instructor of babes for Christ.

When we come to deal with others, earnestly longing to instruct them for Jesus, we perceive even more clearly our need of the Spirit of God. You think you will put the Gospel so clearly that they *must* see it; but their blind eyes overcome you. Ah! you think you will put it so zealously that they *must* feel it; but their clay-cold hearts defeat you. You may think you are going to win souls by your pleadings, but you might as well stand on the top of a mountain and whistle to the wind, unless the Holy Spirit be with you. After all your talking, your hearers will, perhaps, have caught *your* idea, but the mind of the Spirit, the real soul of the Gospel, you cannot impart to them; this remains, like creation itself, a work which only God can accomplish. Daily, then, let us pray for the power of the Spirit as the Illuminator. Come, O blessed light of God! thou alone canst break our personal darkness, and only when thou hast enlightened us can we lead others in thy light.

Thirdly, one work of the Spirit of God is to create in believers the spirit of ADOPTION. "Because ye are sons, God hath sent forth the Spirit of his Son into your hearts, whereby ye cry, Abba, Father!" "For ye have not received the spirit of bondage again to fear, but ye have received the Spirit of adoption, whereby we cry, Abba, Father!" We are regenerated by the Holy Spirit, and so receive the nature of children; and that nature, which is given by him, he continually prompts, and excites, and develops, and matures; so that we receive day by day more and more of the child-like spirit. Now, beloved, this may not seem to you to be of very great importance at first sight; but it is so; for the Church is never happy except as all her members walk as dear children towards God. Sometimes the spirit of slaves creeps over us: we begin to talk of the service of God as though it were heavy and burdensome, and are discontented if we do not receive present wages and visible success, just as servants do when they are not suited; but the spirit of adoption works for love, without any hope of reward, and it is satisfied with the sweet fact of being in the Father's house, and doing the Father's will. This spirit gives peace, rest, joy, boldness, and holy familiarity with God. A man who never received the spirit of a child towards God does not know the bliss of the Christian life; he misses its flower, its savour, its excellence, and I should not wonder if the service of Christ should be a weariness to him because he has never yet got to the sweet things, and does not enjoy the green pastures, wherein the Good Shepherd makes his sheep to feed and to lie down. But when the Spirit of God makes us feel that we are sons, and we live in the house of God to go no more out for ever, then the service of God is sweet and easy, and we accept the delay of apparent success as a part of the trial we are called to bear.

Now, mark you, this will have a great effect upon the outside world. Bring me a Church made up of children of God, a company of men and women whose faces shine with their heavenly Father's smile, who are accustomed to take their cares and cast them on their Father as children should, who know they are accepted and beloved, and are perfectly content with the great Father's will; put them down in the midst of a company of ungodly ones, and I will warrant you they will begin to envy them their peace and joy. Thus happy saints become most efficient operators upon the minds of the unsaved.

Fourthly, the Holy Spirit is especially called the Spirit of HOLINESS. He never suggested sin nor approved of it, nor has he ever done otherwise than grieve over it: but holiness is the Spirit's delight. The Church of God wears upon her brow the words, "Holiness to the Lord." Only in proportion as she is holy may she claim to be the Church of God at all. An unholy Church! Surely this cannot be her of whom we read, "Christ also loved the church, and gave himself for it; that he might sanctify and cleanse it with the washing of water by the word, that he might present it to himself a glorious church, not having spot, or wrinkle, or any such thing." Holiness is not mere morality, not the outward keeping of divine precepts out of a hard sense of duty, while those commandments in themselves are not delightful to us. Holiness is the entirety of our manhood fully consecrated to the Lord and moulded to his will. This is the thing which the Church of God must have, but it can never have it apart from the Sanctifier, for there is not a grain of holiness beneath the sky but what is of the operation of the Holy Ghost.

After all, the acts of the Church preach more to the world than the words of the Church. Put an anointed man to preach the gospel in the midst of a really godly people and his testimony will be marvellously supported by the Church with which he labours; but place the most faithful minister over an ungodly Church, and he has such a weight upon him that he must first clear himself of it, or he cannot succeed. He may preach his heart out, he may pray till his knees are weary, but conversions will be sorely hindered, if indeed they occur at all. There is no likelihood of victory to Israel while Achan's curse is on the camp. An unholy Church makes Christ to say that he cannot do many mighty works there because of its iniquity.

Do you not see in this point our need of the Spirit of God? And when you get to grappling terms with sinners, and have to talk to them about the necessity of holiness, and a renewed heart, and a godly life coming out of that renewed heart, do you expect ungodly men to be charmed with what you say? What cares the unregenerate mind for righteousness? Was a carnal man ever eager after holiness? Such a thing was never seen. As well expect the devil to be in love with God as an unredeemed heart to be in love with holiness. But yet the sinner must love that which is pure and right, or he cannot enter heaven. *You* cannot make him do so. Who can do it but that Holy Ghost who has made you to love what once you also despised? Go not out, therefore, to battle with sin until you have taken weapons out of the armoury of the Eternal Spirit.

Fifthly, the Church needs much PRAYER, and the Holy Spirit is the Spirit of grace and of supplications. The strength of a Church may pretty accurately be gauged by her prayerfulness. We cannot expect God to put forth his power unless we entreat him so to do. Our great High Priest will put into his censer no incense but that which the Spirit has compounded. Prayer is the creation of the Holy Ghost. We cannot do without prayer, and we cannot pray without the Holy Spirit; and hence our dependence on him.

Furthermore, when we come to deal with sinners, we know that they must pray. "Behold he prayeth" is one of the earliest signs of the new birth. But can *we* make the sinner pray? Can any persuasion of ours lead him to his knees to breathe the penitential sigh and look to Christ for mercy? If you have attempted the conversion of a soul in your own strength you know you have failed; and so you would have failed if you had attempted the creation of one single acceptable prayer in the heart of even a little child. Oh then, let us cry to our heavenly Father to give the Holy Spirit to us; let us ask him to be in us more and more mightily as the spirit of prayer, making intercession in us with groanings that cannot be uttered, that the Church may not miss the divine blessing for lack of asking for it. I do verily believe this to be her present weakness, and one great cause why the kingdom of Christ does not more mightily spread: prayer is too much restrained, and hence the blessing is kept back; and it will always be restrained unless the Holy Ghost shall stimulate the desires of his people. O blessed Spirit, we pray thee make us pray, for Jesus' sake.

Sixthly, the Spirit of God is in a very remarkable manner the giver of FELLOWSHIP. So often as we pronounce the apostolic benediction we pray that we may receive the communion of the Holy Ghost. The Holy Ghost enables us to have communion with spiritual things. He alone can take the key and open up the secret mystery, that we may know the things which be of God. He gives us fellowship with God himself: through Jesus Christ by the Spirit we have access to the Father. Our fellowship is with the Father and with his Son Jesus Christ, but it is the Spirit of God who brings us into communion with the Most High. So, too, our fellowship with one another, so far as it is Christian fellowship, is always produced by the Spirit of God. If we have continued together in peace and love these many years, I cannot attribute it to our constitutional good tempers, nor to wise management, nor to any natural causes, but to the love into which the Spirit has baptized us, so that rebellious nature has been still. If a dozen Christian people live together for twelve months in true spiritual union and unbroken affection, trace it to the love of the Spirit; and if a dozen hundred, or four times that number, shall be able to persevere in united service, and find themselves loving each other better after many years than they did at the first, let it be regarded as a blessing from the Comforter, for which he is to be devoutly adored. Fellowship can only come to us by the Spirit, but a Church without fellowship would be a disorderly mob, a kingdom divided against itself, and consequently it could not prosper. You need fellowship for mutual strength, guidance, help, and encouragement, and without it your Church is a mere human society. Let us daily cry to him to work in us brotherly love, and all the sweet graces which make us one with Christ, that we all may be one even as the Father is one with the Son, that the world may know that God hath indeed sent Jesus, and that we are his people.

Seventhly, we need the Holy Spirit in that renowned office which is described by our Lord as THE PARACLETE, or Comforter. The word bears another rendering, which our translators have given to it in that passage where we read, "If any man sin we have an advocate (or Paraclete) with the Father." The Holy Spirit is both Comforter and Advocate.

The Holy Spirit at this present moment is our friend and *Comforter*, sustaining the sinking spirits of believers, applying the precious promises, revealing the love of Jesus Christ to the heart. Many a heart would break if the Spirit of God had not comforted it. Many of God's dear children would have utterly died by the way if he had not bestowed upon them his divine consolations to cheer their pilgrimage. That is his work, and a very necessary work, for if believers become unhappy they become weak for many points of service. I am certain that the joy of the Lord is our strength, for I have proved it so, and proved also the opposite truth. There are on earth certain Christians who inculcate gloom as a Christian's proper state, I will not judge them, but this I will say, that in evangelistic work they do nothing, and I do not wonder. Till snow in harvest ripens wheat, till darkness makes flowers blossom, till the salt sea yields clusters bursting with new wine, you will never find an unhappy religion promotive of the growth of the kingdom of Christ. You must have joy in the Lord, if you are to be strong *in* the Lord, and strong *for* the Lord. Now, as the Comforter alone can bear you up amid the floods of tribulation which you are sure to meet with, you see your great need of his consoling presence.

We have said that the Spirit of God is the *Advocate* of the Church—not with God, for there Christ is our sole Advocate—but with man. What is the grandest plea that the Church has against the world? I answer, the indwelling of the Holy Ghost, the standing miracle of the Church. External evidences are very excellent. You young men who are worried by sceptics will do well to study those valuable works which learned and devout men have with much labour produced for us, but, mark you, all the evidences of the truth of Christianity which can be gathered from analogy, from history, and from external facts, are nothing whatever compared with the operations of the Spirit of God. These are the arguments which convince.

A man says to me, "I do not believe in sin, in righteousness, or in judgment." Well, the Holy Ghost can soon convince him. If he asks me for signs and evidences of the truth of the Gospel, I reply, "Seest thou this woman; she was a great sinner in the very worst sense, and led others into sin, but now you cannot find more sweetness and light anywhere than in her. Hearest thou this profane swearer, persecutor, and blasphemer? He is speaking with purity, truth, and humbleness of mind. Observe yon man, who was aforetime a miser, and see how he consecrates his substance. Notice that envious, malicious spirit, and see how it becomes gentle, forgiving, and amiable through conversion.

How do you account for these great changes? They are happening here every day, how come they to pass? Is that a lie which produces truth, honesty, and love? Does not every tree bear fruit after its kind? What then must that grace be which produces such blessed transformations? The wonderful phenomena of ravens turned to doves, and lions into lambs, the marvellous transformations of moral character which the minister of Christ rejoices to see wrought by the Gospel, these are our witnesses, and they are unanswerable. Peter and John have gone up to the temple, and they have healed a lame man; they are soon seized and brought before the Sanhedrim. This is the charge against them—"You have been preaching in the name of Jesus, and this Jesus is an impostor." What do Peter and John say? They need say nothing, for there stands the man that was healed; he has brought his crutch with him, and he waves it in triumph, and he runs and leaps. He was their volume of evidences, their apology, and proof. "When they saw the man that was healed standing with Peter and John, they could say nothing against them."

If we have the Spirit of God amongst us, and conversions are constantly being wrought, the Holy Spirit is thus fulfilling his advocacy, and refuting all accusers. If the Spirit works in your own mind, it will always be to you the best evidence of the Gospel. I meet sometimes one piece of infidelity, and then another; for there are new doubts and fresh infidelities spawned every hour, and unstable men expect us to read all the books they choose to produce. But the effect produced on our mind is less and less. This is our answer. It is of no use your trying to stagger us, for we are already familiar with everything you suggest; our own native unbelief has outstripped you. We have had doubts of a kind which even you would not dare to utter if you knew them; for there is enough infidelity and devilry in our own nature to make us no strangers to Satan's devices. We have fought most of your suggested battles over and over again in the secret chamber of our meditation and have conquered. For *we have been in personal contact with God.* You sneer, but there is no argument in sneering. We are as honest as you are, and our witness is as good as yours in any court of law; and we solemnly declare that we have felt the power of the Holy Spirit over our soul as much as ever old ocean has felt the force of the north wind: we have been stirred to agony under a sense of sin, and we have been lifted to ecstasy of delight by faith in the righteousness of Christ. We find that in the little world within our soul the Lord Jesus manifests himself so that we know him. There is a potency about the doctrines we have learned which could not belong to lies, for the truths which we believe we have tested in actual experience. Tell us there is no such thing as light? We do not know how we can prove its existence to you, for you are probably blind, but *we* can see. That is enough argument for us, and our witness is true. Tell us there is no spiritual life! We feel it in our inmost souls. These are the answers with which the Spirit of God furnishes us, and they are a part of his advocacy.

See, again, how entirely dependent we are on the Spirit of God for meeting all the various forms of unbelief which arise around us; you may have your societies for collecting evidence, and you may enlist all your bishops and doctors of divinity and professors of apologetics, and they may write rolls of evidence long enough to girdle the globe, but the only person who can savingly convince the world is the Advocate whom the Father has sent in the name of Jesus. When he reveals a man's sin, and the sure result of it, the unbeliever takes to his knees. When he takes away the scales and sets forth the crucified Redeemer, and the merit of the precious blood, all carnal reasonings are nailed to the Cross. One blow of real conviction of sin will stagger the most obstinate unbeliever, and afterwards, if his unbelief return, the Holy Ghost's consolations will soon comfort it out of him. Therefore, as at the first so say I at the last, all this dependeth upon the Holy Ghost, and upon him let us wait in the name of Jesus, beseeching him to manifest his power among us.